TWO BANDRA GIRLS BUY A FARM

ARTI DWARKADAS

TWO BANDRA GIRLS BUY A FARM

Chaos, Community and Crops in Rural Maharashtra

WESTLAND
NON·FICTION

WESTLAND
NON·FICTION

Published by Westland Non-Fiction, an imprint of Westland Books, a division of Nasadiya Technologies Private Limited, in 2026

No. 269/2B, First Floor, 'Irai Arul', Vimalraj Street, Nethaji Nagar, Alapakkam Main Road, Maduravoyal, Chennai 600095

ISBN: 9789371977760

10 9 8 7 6 5 4 3 2 1

Typeset by Mukul

Printed at Parksons Graphics Pvt. Ltd

'To forget how to dig the earth and tend the soil is to forget ourselves.'

Mahatma Gandhi

'If you wish to know the divine, feel the wind on your face and the sun on your hands.'

Buddha

'He who plants a tree, plants a hope.'

Lucy Larcom

For Mum,
who left too soon

Contents

Prologue

My mum had the greenest thumb. Our home wasn't just filled with plants—it was consumed by them. Vines draped themselves dramatically over bookshelves, pots lined every available surface, and ferns peeked out from unexpected corners like mischievous guests who had overstayed their welcome. The air was thick with the scent of damp earth, mingling with the crisp, peppery bite of crushed leaves. Our house was less a home and more a living, breathing jungle, and I wouldn't have had it any other way.

Mum's relationship with plants was less of a hobby and more of a quiet, steadfast devotion. She had an uncanny ability to revive anything, from drooping hibiscus to stubborn cuttings that had no business surviving. She was a miracle worker, coaxing life from the most reluctant of roots. My earliest memories are of her sitting cross-legged on the floor, surrounded by a fortress of potted plants, pruning, whispering and gently reshaping her beloved bonsais. Those miniature trees weren't just plants to her—they were lessons in patience, care and discipline. She would trim them with the precision of an artist, guiding each tiny branch as if sculpting a masterpiece.

In many ways, she raised us, her three daughters, the same way she raised her plants. She let us grow wild but shaped us with a firm yet gentle hand. She knew when to support, when to step back, and when a little tough love was necessary to ensure we didn't end up sprawling in all the wrong directions.

I inherited her love for nurturing things, though certainly not her discipline. Where Mum created a sanctuary, I created a riot. My so-called 'kitchen garden' on my Bandra balconies was a chaotic, edible jungle.

Flowers were lovely, yes, but if a plant couldn't be tossed into a pan or a salad bowl, it held little appeal. What began as a modest herb garden quickly spiralled into something far more ambitious. Tomatoes climbed over the railings, jostling with unruly chilli, while spinach popped up in mismatched pots and basil quietly elbowed its way into every available corner.

The kitchen garden quickly outgrew its name and became a full-blown food jungle. I didn't just grow vegetables, I waged daily battles with them. Some thrived spectacularly, others refused to cooperate and a few seemed determined to wither out of sheer spite.

Garden centres became my personal wonderland. I would spend hours poring over seed packets, imagining the possibilities with the kind of enthusiasm most people reserved for vacations. There was something intoxicating about the idea of growing food, of turning tiny seeds into thriving, edible abundance. It felt like magic—messy, unpredictable and exhilarating.

Then the world changed, and so did my connection to growing things.

When the pandemic hit, my chaotic balcony garden became my sanctuary. Outside, the world ground to a halt, but within my jungle of pots, life continued. My plants neither knew nor cared about lockdowns. They just kept growing, oblivious to the uncertainty swirling around us. I, in turn, poured myself into tending them with the same urgency with which I had once tackled deadlines and commutes. Somewhere along the way, the hobby stopped being a pastime and became a refuge.

Before I knew it, I was harvesting more than I knew what to do with. Bottle gourds hung heavily from the vines. Spinach, amaranth, radishes, chillies and even a few determined guavas made an appearance. At one point, I half-joked about setting up a mini produce stall outside my building, except that it wasn't entirely a joke—I genuinely had more than I could consume. The abundance felt like a message I hadn't yet learnt how to interpret.

And then I received a phone call and was asked a single question: would I be interested in buying farmland?

I should have hesitated, mulled it over, made pro-and-con lists, consulted financial spreadsheets. Instead, I heard myself say, 'Yes.'

Looking back now, I understand why that yes came so easily. The world had shrunk, and everything felt stagnant except for the plants growing steadily in front of me. Maybe it was monotony. Maybe it was longing. Or maybe, deep down, I was following the quiet tug of Mum's lessons—towards soil, growth and possibility.

Going from a city balcony garden to full-scale farming might seem like an outrageous leap. But to me, it felt like the natural extension of an obsession that had been quietly taking hold for years. Yes, it brought its share of wild misadventures—bureaucratic mazes, bovine ambushes, and a cast of characters I couldn't have invented if I tried. But it never felt impulsive. The farm became more than a piece of land; it became a place where I kept growing too—not just plants, but ideas, possibilities, and a version of myself I didn't yet know.

This is the story of how two city girls—and one deeply sceptical husband—traded balcony pots for muddy boots, swapped Google searches for real-life farming mishaps, and discovered that sometimes, the wildest leaps aren't leaps at all. They're just the next step in a journey that was waiting all along.

YEAR ONE: LATE 2020–21

1

The 'Yes' Heard Across Bandra

November 2020–January 2021

IT BEGAN WITH A SINGLE WORD—RECKLESS, DEFIANT AND utterly life-changing.

'Yes.'

One morning in November 2020, crouched on my Bandra balcony, I plucked yet another handful of smugly red chillies and faced an unsettling truth: I had officially run out of people to burden with my organic overachievements. The fridge was a wasteland of wilting arugula and spinach multiplying like bacteria in a petri dish. My friends—once enthusiastic recipients—had started avoiding my calls. Even the building's watchman, who never turned down food, politely suggested I 'try someone else'.

I stared at the latest harvest, wondering what on earth I was going to do with it. And then my phone rang.

It was Suzann—my husband Sunil's friend and former colleague. She didn't bother with small talk. 'I have an idea,' she said. 'A big one.'

Given our shared history of questionable ideas, I knew better than to expect anything reasonable. 'Okay ...'

'I want to buy farmland. Go organic. Grow our own food. Sustainability. You in?'

I should have paused. I should have asked grown-up questions like:

Where is this land? Who will farm it? Do we even know what topsoil is? But I didn't. Because sometimes, your inner voice is drowned out by the sound of too many chillies hitting the sink.

'Yes,' I said, before my brain could intervene.

Across the room, Sunil, mid-sip of coffee, choked. 'You what?'

'I said yes,' I repeated, as if repetition made it more rational. 'To farming. Buying land. Growing food. Living off the land.' I gestured vaguely at our balcony—potted chaos where basil strangled mint and tomato vines attempted escape over the railing. 'It's practically the same thing.'

Sunil stared. 'You have five basil plants and a psychotic chilli bush. That's not farming.'

He had a point. But something in Suzann's excitement had already hooked me—the promise of doing something bigger in our tiny, pandemic-shrunk worlds. Something messier, earthier, more alive than the narrow rhythms my days had settled into.

Suzann continued: acreage, organic methods, water sources, possibilities—words that sounded thrilling and terrifying in equal measure.

'So,' she said finally, 'should I move ahead?'

Apparently, I already had.

'Yes,' said again, sealing our collective fate.

And just like that, the first domino fell.

Suzann took my yes and ran with it. She had a plan. We'd scout land, get farmer certificates, figure the rest out as we went. She spoke with the breezy confidence of someone suggesting a weekend pottery class, not a complete life overhaul.

In a world where every day had started feeling the same, her absurd plan had an undeniable pull. The idea of doing something real, something grounded and unpredictable, was strangely exhilarating.

A few days later, masked and socially distanced, we met to finalise what was clearly a completely irrational decision. Suzann and I were all in. Sunil, still sceptical, hovered somewhere between amusement and alarm.

Suzann appointed herself the 'Chief Land Scout' with the zeal of someone on a mission from the gods of sustainable living. Each weekend, she plotted ambitious routes on Google Maps, packed enough snacks to survive a minor apocalypse and set off at dawn in search of the perfect plot. Her travels took her through sugarcane fields, sleepy villages, hillocks cloaked in mist and endless tea stalls serving suspiciously watery chai. She crisscrossed Maharashtra, clocking thousands of kilometres and collecting tales of near-misses, wrong turns and occasionally helpful brokers. Her weekly updates arrived in brisk, bullet-pointed texts that read like cryptic postcards from a parallel universe:

- Too hilly
- No proper access

- The kind of place where someone could emerge from the bushes with a machete
- Has a distinctly haunted air

Haunted?

She wasn't joking. The place had a strange energy—an eerie silence, a weight in the air. Even the broker was jumpy. And just like that, 'vibes' joined our list of property criteria.

Then, one Saturday in January, Suzann called, breathless. 'Two plots near Kolad. Seven kilometres apart. They're perfect.'

On 31 January 2021, we drove to Kolad, a town better known for white-water rafting than agriculture. The drive took us past roadside temples draped in marigolds, bullock carts stacked high with bananas, and narrow bridges that creaked under our wheels. The road coiled through the countryside, and as we left the last petrol pump behind, signal bars disappeared from our phones like breadcrumbs dropped into the forest.

The journey along NH66 unspooled through rolling greens, patchwork fields, rivers snaking past rocky outcrops. Even the air changed—less exhaust, more wet earth. For a moment, it felt like we were drifting into another world.

Suzann was practically buzzing with anticipation. Sunil remained unconvinced, quietly calculating suspension damage with every jolt. I sat somewhere in between, caught between adventure and anxiety.

We stopped for Kolad's famous misal pav, a fiery explosion of flavour that burnt all the way down. Sunil, wiping his forehead, muttered that if farming didn't work out, we could always come back for the food.

Re-energised, we followed the broker off the highway onto a dirt trail that barely qualified as a road. It wasn't on Google Maps.

It wasn't really a road. It was eight kilometres of baked mud, loose rock and existential doubt—carved into the wilderness by little more than habit and hope. We were off-grid, off-map and quite possibly off our rockers. As we bumped along through rising dust and clawing branches, Sunil exhaled, 'The car isn't making it back in one piece.'

After a bone-rattling ride, we reached Mahagaon Adivasi village. The rest of the road was unmotorable, so we abandoned the car and walked, dodging rocks, ducking branches and wondering if this was some kind of endurance test.

The broker, a talkative man with a constantly animated face, led us through a scattering of huts patched with makeshift repairs. Children peered at us before vanishing with laughter into the trees. The landscape grew wilder—scraggly mango trees, overgrown bushes, weeds everywhere.

Finally, said broker gestured grandly at a sloping, untamed stretch of land. It was dense with weeds, half-shaded by unruly cashew trees, and sloped just enough to make you wonder where your balance—or your dreams—might go rolling. The only real sign of life was a suspiciously alert goat chewing thoughtfully under a mango tree, as if she'd been waiting for someone to ask her opinion on soil fertility. It didn't feel perfect. There was no cinematic swell of music, no rush of emotion, no instant knowing. I wasn't swept away by awe or struck by a sense of destiny. Instead, I found myself blinking at a piece of land that looked like it had never known a plan or a plough—only the occasional visits from a bored goat and a broker with dramatic hand gestures and an animated face. Just dust in our mouths, sweat on our backs, and a creeping realisation that we had left the world of Google Maps far behind. It felt remote, wild and slightly intimidating—a place that made you question whether you could ever belong there or you would always remain city people who had simply followed a half-baked dream into the jungle.

Suzann turned to me, glowing. 'It's good, isn't it?'

Everything in me said, 'Turn back.' The land was wild, unfamiliar and utterly indifferent to our city-bred optimism. But against all logic and reason, I nodded.

There was no thunderclap, no music swell—just a dust-filled silence and the uncomfortable certainty that we were in way over our heads.

In early 2021, with the world unravelling, it almost made sense to say yes to something so unpredictable.

'Yes.'

2

Land, Lawyers and Lunacy

February–March 2021

THAT RECKLESS 'YES' ECHOED LOUDER WITH EACH passing step. What had started as a whimsical response to too many chillies and not enough freezer space had now become the drumbeat beneath every bewildering move we made—from navigating farmer certificates to falling down Google rabbit holes about soil types at 2 a.m., we had no clue where this adventure was heading. But that one impulsive 'yes' had already pushed us off the ledge—and we hadn't stopped tumbling since.

And now, thanks to that single syllable, we found ourselves perched on a sagging sofa, about to sign a document that would tie us to a patch of land we barely understood. The broker's living room, where we signed the MOU, felt frozen in the

1980s—floral sofas, dusty display cabinets, incense hanging in the air. The documents felt oddly underwhelming, considering they were about to redefine our lives.

We also met what would soon become the yin and yang of our farming journey. The 'Farm Friend', who looked like he hadn't moved in a decade, radiated calm detachment and the quiet patience of someone who had seen too many city folk try and fail. And then there was the 'Farm Fiend', who talked like a radio host on speed, buzzing with ideas, promises and the unshakeable confidence of a man who could probably build a shed out of mango peels and twine if left unsupervised. He could manage it all, he promised—tools, workers, even a dancing cow. We nodded, naive and optimistic.

And then we met Maharashtra's beloved bureaucracy.

To buy farmland, we needed a farmer's certificate—a document more elusive than a unicorn. In Tamil Nadu, farmland could be bought with ease. Here, it required proof of agricultural lineage, as though we were applying for admission into an ancient guild.

It was like getting a Hogwarts letter—but instead of a castle full of magic, we were drafted into the Ministry of Paperwork, where the favourite spell was 'Fill out this form in triplicate'. What followed was a marathon through dusty corridors, echoing stamps, and a hydra of paperwork—every time we completed a sheet, three more grew in its place. After weeks of stubbornness—and enough red tape to gift-wrap a tractor—we finally got the certificate.

Now that we were legally able to purchase land, we turned to the next task: construction. But building a farmhouse in such remote terrain was a logistical nightmare. The cost alone was daunting, rivalled only by the frustration of trying to catch a network signal that vanished the moment you so much as thought about making a call. The land's isolation was almost mythical—if a rakshasa had stepped out from behind the trees to complain about the heat, I might have asked if he had better reception. Even sending a basic text required a dance around the field, phone held aloft like an offering to the gods of connectivity. But connectivity, as it turned out, wasn't our only enemy. The journey there had its own special brand of torture.

The road to our farm wasn't a road—it was a cosmic endurance test. Each journey was accompanied by the relentless crunch of tyres on loose gravel, the jarring thuds of unsuspecting potholes, and the occasional startled squawk of a bird that had miscalculated its flight path. A true symphony of rural chaos. A gauntlet of despair. A place where hubcaps went to die. Each trip was a brutal lesson in patience, suspension strength and the laws of physics, particularly the ones that dictate what happens when you hit a crater-sized pothole at thirty kilometres per hour. Imagine attempting an obstacle course designed by a particularly vindictive mountain god—where the hurdles are jagged rocks, the potholes could double as tiger traps and the local goats operate under an unwavering belief that they own the right of way.

And just as your spine contemplated early retirement and your faith in suspension systems evaporated, you crested the final hill. And there it was—the farm. A patchwork of greens and browns, kissed by sunlight, whispering, *See? Worth it.* And for a brief, blissful moment, you almost believed it. Almost.

Nestled at 250 metres above sea level, the farm rests in the foothills of the Western Ghats—an ancient range with a flair for drama. Older than the Himalayas and born of Gondwana's slow unravelling, these mountains wear their age openly. Their slopes are unpredictable, offering a mix of breathtaking vistas and simmering hostility. They temper the monsoon's fury, soaking up rain like a sponge, while also conspiring against us with rocky, stubborn soil that turns farming into an elaborate puzzle.

When we first saw the land, it was less 'fertile farmland' and more 'thicket of doom'. A narrow dirt village road sliced through the middle of the property—a feature the broker insisted was 'very convenient'. What it actually was, we later realised, was a logistical nightmare: doubling our fencing costs, complicating irrigation and ensuring that no task would ever be simple. The so-called 'flat' area, advertised as perfect for paddy, was only flat in the way that a mildly deflated football is flat.

By then, it had become painfully clear that this was not the kind of land where you built a charming farmhouse and hosted languid weekend brunches. This was the kind of land that required grit, resourcefulness and a tolerance for chaos. So instead of forcing a picture-perfect dream onto a terrain that clearly had other plans, we pivoted to day trips and saved the farmhouse fantasy for a future, better-prepared version of ourselves.

That decision set off a new quest: finding a farm car—something sturdy enough to tackle the terrain, haul equipment and not bankrupt us. A mechanical unicorn, essentially.

We were inching forward, clueless but committed.

Until, of course, the seller left the country.

Just like that. No warning, no explanation. One day she was part of the process, the next she was on a flight out.

The registration was already scheduled, but with her sudden disappearance, we had no choice but to push it by fifteen days. The new date: 17 March 2021.

And then, on the eve of the registration, came the next twist.

The broker called, sounding far too calm for someone delivering bad news. 'The registrar won't accept the sale deed in English,' he said. 'It has to be in Marathi.'

Overnight.

Because legal translations are just the sort of thing one can whip up in a few hours between dinner and bedtime. Panic flickered in Suzann's eyes. For a moment, we pictured ourselves hunched over Google Translate, attempting to decode legal jargon in a language we barely grasped. Hereby referred to as the first party—Pahilya Pakshane—no, wait, was that even right? The absurdity of it all made us dizzy. And yet, beneath the panic, there was a flicker of determination—the kind that usually precedes either great adventure or spectacular disaster. Thankfully, our lawyer, Mr Sanap, was unflappable. 'They're messing with you,' he said.

He was right.

At the Tala Sub-Registrar's office, we were welcomed by flickering tube lights and the lingering scent of sweat and onion pakodas.

The seller was late. Very late. Our patience was wearing thin. Noticing our restlessness, the broker took it upon himself to fill the silence—with a spontaneous lecture on virology.

'Corona?' he scoffed. 'That's only in big cities where people sit in AC comfort all day!' Rural Maharashtra was of course an impenetrable fortress against the virus, where hard work, sweat and hours of sunshine bestowed immunity like some agricultural superhero serum.

Suzann and I exchanged glances and kept our masks firmly on, partly because we were the only ones wearing them and partly because, as city folk, we weren't blessed with the superhero immunity that seemed to come free with rural Maharashtra.

The whole exchange would have been almost funny, but this was March 2021, a full year after the first lockdown and just a month before the second wave would crash into rural Maharashtra like a tsunami, sudden and relentless, leaving devastation in its wake. The nonchalance in his voice felt surreal, but at that moment, we had other concerns.

Time oozed past like the registrar's ceiling fan—slow, uneven and oddly resigned to its fate. Somewhere in that languid haze, we learnt the seller and her retired government-officer father had managed to get themselves lost. Then, just as mysteriously, they were found—only to refuse to step out of their car.

We refused to go to them. A silent standoff followed.

Eventually, she arrived, stepping out of a car with curtained windows as if she were smuggling state secrets rather than showing up for a routine legal formality. She had come without Aadhaar, without photos, without a single sheet of paperwork—as though bringing essential documents to a registration appointment was terribly pedestrian.

What followed was part scavenger hunt, part street theatre: one person dashed off to retrieve ID scans, another squinted at a crumbling wall to see if it could pass for a photo studio backdrop, and someone else sprinted off in search of a printer, likely bartering a vada pav and a prayer to coax it into functioning.

Finally, the documents were signed. Sweets were exchanged—awkwardly, like diplomats sealing an uneasy truce.

Her car, curtains still tightly drawn to ensure aristocratic opacity, lingered in the compound just long enough for one final, inexplicable flourish: the trunk popped open to receive offerings from random persons who had apparently been collecting vegetables, fish and a few jackfruit for this exact moment. They approached quietly, placed their contributions with care and walked away without a word. The car disappeared in a swirl of dust, like a magician's final trick.

Thirty more minutes. We had the deed in our hands.

Just like that, we owned land.

No water. No electricity. No access road. Not even a working tap or a single square foot of cleared earth to call ours. Only a wild, tangled sprawl humming with insects and madness and the reckless belief that we might coax something into growing there.

Driving back to Mumbai, the exhaustion gave way to something quieter.

Suzann stared out the window. 'This land ... it's pulling something out of me I didn't know was there.'

I didn't answer immediately. In the silence, the day replayed itself—rural virology theories, lost sellers and jackfruit trades and curtained cars. It all felt like a fever dream, equal parts comedy and chaos. But underneath the absurdity, something had shifted.

I felt it too—that strange, magnetic pull. The sense that we hadn't just bought land, we'd been claimed by it. As though the soil had been waiting, patiently, for two clueless city people to stumble in and be transformed. This wasn't just an escape from the lockdown. It was a transformation already in motion. The road ahead was bumpy, uncertain—and entirely ours.

We had no farm plan. No planting calendar. No idea what soil pH even meant. But we had paperwork, blind faith and an alarming number of WhatsApp forwards about composting.

The real adventure hadn't just begun. It had grabbed us by the ankles and dragged us, kicking and googling, into the mud.

3

The Fiend and the Satbara Saga

April 2021

OWNERSHIP, IT TURNED OUT, WAS ONLY THE BEGINNING.

We were about to step into the enigmatic realm of the 7/12 Utara, a document whose very name evoked the incantations of an ancient cult. Affectionately known as the 'Satbara', which literally means 7/12 in Marathi, this document is the ultimate authority in Maharashtra's rural land records. It details everything about a piece of land—from ownership history and tenancy claims to the crops grown and any government acquisitions or restrictions. If a property had ever been mortgaged or mired in legal disputes, the Satbara would reveal it all. It is both a badge of honour and a bureaucratic nightmare.

The 7/12 extract is essentially your land's destiny written on a single sheet of paper. Form 7 lists ownership details, including ancestral claims and potential inheritance disputes. Form 12, on the other hand, documents agricultural aspects like soil type, water sources and even government schemes the land is entangled in. It can also contain hidden surprises, like a provision for grazing rights for wandering cattle or sudden government reservations that could derail farming dreams overnight.

Paying for the land and registering the sale deed, we quickly learnt, was only the first step. What followed was the far less celebratory task of getting our names entered into the 7/12 records. This process, overseen by the Revenue Department, required saintly patience, a fresh stack of passport photos, a folder full of notarised documents and the ability to decipher Marathi legalese that appeared to have been carbon copied since the time of Shivaji.

Our broker, a man who existed in a permanent state of half-truths and exaggerated promises, assured us he would 'handle everything'. We quickly discovered this was code for 'I'll take your money and occasionally appear with updates that mean nothing'.

Once we had handed over the sale deed to kickstart the process of securing our Satbara, we turned our attention to the land itself. And that's when we realised that owning land doesn't automatically mean you can access it. As we'd realised when we first saw the farm, there was no way to drive up to it; we had to park in the nearby Adivasi hamlet and trudge the last 300 metres. There was no proper access road, just an uneven path that could barely accommodate a bicycle. It seemed the rural road authorities had decided that infrastructure was overrated and that adventure should be mandatory with every visit.

Also, we needed a government survey because, apparently, just knowing where the land was wasn't enough. A boundary survey was necessary, if only to inform the neighbour's goats where to stop snacking. A fence had to be built, strong enough to keep out livestock, overly curious villagers and possibly our own creeping doubts.

Water was another hurdle. We were told to find a water diviner—a suggestion that sounded more like a plot device from folklore than a serious logistical solution. Electricity would require bureaucratic sweet-talking and relentless grovelling. A farm consultant was needed to help us plan and plant, because turning six acres of wild land into a flourishing farm required more than just wishful thinking. Farm labour had to be found, because no matter how enthusiastic we were, we simply couldn't plough the fields ourselves. And if our future caretaker turned out to be from outside the local area, we would have to build them a house to ensure they wouldn't flee at the first sight of our underdeveloped infrastructure.

With an evergrowing to-do list and no idea of where to begin, we realised we needed help—local, reliable and preferably patient. We met Mahesh just a few weeks after signing the sale deed, when our search for a reliable water diviner led us straight to him. A local legend who seemed to know everyone and everything in the region, he quickly became our unofficial guide. Borewell expert? Chai stop? Directions, contacts, shortcuts, gossip—Mahesh had an answer for everything.

In no time at all, Mahesh found us a water diviner—an older man who arrived with quiet confidence and, to Mahesh's surprise, a coconut. He held it like a sacred relic, and when he claimed it could find water, Mahesh wasn't sure whether to laugh or follow his lead. Turns out, coconuts know things. Mahesh later described how the coconut would suddenly straighten in the dowser's palm, rising to attention as if responding to a secret only the diviner could hear.

Real or not, it identified two possible spots where we could dig for water.

Through Mahesh we were soon introduced to Sanjay, a grim-faced agricultural consultant with the air of a man who had seen it all and wasn't particularly impressed.

While the diviner's coconut-based magic felt like something out of a bedtime story, Grim Sanjay brought us crashing back to reality. He surveyed what we optimistically referred to as our 'farm' with the expression of a man forced to babysit a jungle gone rogue—a tangle of wild mango trees, scraggly bushes and vines that looked ready to launch a coup. It was the kind of thicket that might swallow an unsuspecting farmer whole.

The first thing Sanjay said, after a long, silent walk around the property, was that we should keep the wild mango trees. 'Graft Alphonso onto them,' he said, barely glancing up. 'You'll get a proper harvest in a few years.'

We were all for preserving those trees—after all, who wants to be the villain in a tree-hugging tale? He also pointed out an ideal spot for growing rice, a part of the land we hadn't even thought to explore. With our newfound expertise from Mahesh and Sanjay—affectionately dubbed M&S—we felt like seasoned farmers ready to take on the world.

Later, with a hint of doom and a practised eye, Sanjay surveyed the tangle of bushes and bramble, muttered something about the pointlessness of clearing it by hand, and declared, 'We'll need an excavator.' His tone suggested that anything less would be like trying to mow a football field with a pair of nail clippers. Within days, a yellow behemoth arrived, its metal claw poised to take on the greenery with a vengeance.

Watching the excavator in action was oddly mesmerising. It moved with the frenzied energy of an elephant in musth, wild and unstoppable, its claw-like arm acting as a trunk in full, thrashing motion. Like a crazed tusker, it tore through the underbrush with ruthless efficiency, uprooting trees and flinging them aside as though they were weightless. The excavator seemed to embody the chaos and the power of nature itself, churning up the earth and reshaping the land with each swing. Sanjay stood nearby, arms crossed, directing the chaos with the intensity of a battlefield commander. His sharp eyes tracked every movement of the excavator, scanning for inefficiencies or, worse, outright blunders. Occasionally, he would mutter instructions to the operator, his words clipped and precise, as if the survival of the world's agriculture depended on this very moment. 'Phude! Phude! Stop—STOP! Do you want to uproot the whole farm?' he bellowed, throwing his hands up in exasperation. The operator, an unflappable man who had clearly endured worse critics, merely grunted and adjusted the claw's trajectory.

For Suzann and me, the sight was both thrilling and terrifying. Thrilling because it felt like progress—our unruly jungle was finally taking shape as farmland. Terrifying because the excavator seemed to have a mind of its own, indiscriminately swinging its claw and sending us scrambling for cover more than once. I made a mental note never to stand too close to heavy machinery again.

At one point, the claw came dangerously close to a wild mango tree we had planned to save. 'No, no, no! Not that one!' Suzann shouted, waving her arms frantically. The operator paused, regarded her with an expression of mild curiosity, and then turned to Sanjay, awaiting confirmation. Sanjay sighed, rubbing his temples as if reconsidering all his life choices. 'Fine, leave the bloody tree. But if it blocks the road later, it's on you.'

By the end of the day, the land had been transformed—or at least, a small part of it. What had once been an impenetrable wilderness was now a patchwork of cleared earth and debris. Sanjay stood triumphant in the middle like a grim-faced conqueror surveying his newly claimed territory. 'In a week,' he said, his voice carrying the weight of a thousand harvests, 'we can start planting.'

It was a small victory, yes, but in a journey full of obstacles, even the smallest steps felt monumental. As I watched Sanjay stride purposefully across the newly cleared land, I couldn't help but think, if a coconut can find water, maybe we can actually make this farm work.

Just when we thought we were finding our rhythm, with M&S guiding us with quiet competence and actual solutions, the broker and the Farm Fiend reappeared, the latter a self-appointed fixer and local bully who had attached himself to our farm plans early on. If Mahesh and Sanjay were calm and practical, these two were all showmanship and swagger. They had arrived ready to take charge, armed with a toolbox of buzzwords and a script full of vague promises. What they found instead was a functional team already mid-execution. Expecting confusion, they found control; expecting desperation, they found a plan. Their faces fell. They fumbled to reframe their role—not as rescuers, but as overlooked visionaries whose brilliance had been prematurely dismissed.

Their first tactic was to charm us into abandoning M&S for their 'expert' recommendations, wielding smiles so insincere they could have been rented by the hour. When that failed spectacularly, they shifted gears to full-blown slander, claiming our new allies were nothing more than scheming con artists lying in wait to fleece us. Things took a sharp turn from annoying to outright absurd when the Farm Fiend threatened Mahesh with bodily harm if he so much as set foot on our farm again, claiming he would use his local connections with government offices to bring our 7/12 application to a grinding halt. The air grew thick with tension. Voices rose. Tempers boiled. Before I knew it, I was locked in a shouting match with him.

He waved his finger like an amateur conductor, repeating the threat with theatrical confidence. In a system where paperwork moved at the speed of relationships, it was not an idle one. It was the kind of standoff that made Bollywood drama look like a quiet afternoon in the park.

Mahesh and Sanjay, the wise sages they were, cautioned restraint. 'Don't rock the boat until your name is on that document.'

Mahesh, ever the diplomat, graciously offered to stay away from the farm until the dust settled. It was a wise move, but we hadn't anticipated the ripple effect it would cause. With Mahesh out of the picture, our resident nemesis—the Farm Fiend—saw an opening. He immediately pivoted, adopting a newfound (and entirely unconvincing) air of camaraderie.

What came next was completely out of character. Instead of his usual passive-aggressive manoeuvring, the Fiend boldly unveiled his grand vision with the zeal of a self-declared saviour. Without so much as seeking approval, he commandeered the excavator and proclaimed his plan to build a motorable access road—a 'lifeline', as he described it—from the hamlet to our farm. And so, a road materialised—unsolicited, certainly, but not entirely unnecessary.

He assured us it was all in our best interest, as if he were some sort of benevolent road-building deity. In reality, all he did was steal soil from a neighbouring farm, dump it haphazardly along the path, and then roll over it with a tractor—the same way he'd roll it over our sanity if given half the chance.

When I had the audacity to object to this laughable excuse for road construction, the Fiend turned on me faster than a faulty lawnmower. He threatened to file an official complaint against me for violating some section of the Mines and Minerals Act. I hadn't the faintest clue what that was, but I knew it couldn't be anything good. As if that weren't enough, he stirred up a small village uprising, telling us that the locals didn't take kindly to outsiders. And guess who was their self-appointed spokesperson and mediator? Yes, our very own Farm Fiend. The man was a one-stop shop for chaos.

And each time the Fiend cheerfully added another 'essential' expense, my heart sank a little further. We'd set aside a budget, but watching it steadily drain away felt like a slow bleed. Sure, we hadn't emptied our coffers, but every extra rupee we spent here was one less we could use on other farm essentials.

As for Sanjay—poor, patient Sanjay—he was left twiddling his thumbs, sidelined by the Fiend's grand ambitions. With the excavator monopolised for the so-called roadwork, actual farm tasks were sidelined. And if you think we could just hire another excavator, you couldn't be more wrong. This is *very* rural Maharashtra, where these behemoths are few and far between, and securing one often involves a mix of divine intervention, bribery and sheer luck.

Through it all, Suzann and I clung to our sense of humour like a lifeline. Amid sleepless nights and mounting bills, we often found ourselves asking, 'Why are we doing this?' The answer, though frequently obscured by frustration, was simple: we believed in the dream of this farm. If that meant navigating the chaos of rural bureaucracy and surviving the Fiend's antics, so be it. After all, who could have predicted we'd end up building highways and dodging mining violations under the reign of the Farm Fiend?

But even lifelines can fray, and when the weight of it all became too much—when we were completely exasperated and teetering on the edge of insanity—I finally caved and called in reinforcements. Enter Sunil's cousin, who called a friend, who, in turn, introduced me to the personal assistant of one of Maharashtra's political heavyweights. This wasn't some quaint rural network; it was the kind of urban power play that hinges on knowing the right people in the right circles. Before I knew it, I was on the phone with this enigmatic assistant. Sympathetic yet brutally honest, he didn't sugarcoat the reality: 'Local goons? Par for the course in Raigad. Even if I manage to shoo away your Farm Fiend, another one will pop up faster than you can plant your next crop.'

Oh, and if that wasn't discouraging enough, he also suggested we sell the land and abandon this little 'hobie'—yes, that's 'hobby' with a generous sprinkle of condescension. But if we were determined to stick with farming, he had a brilliant piece of advice: make friends with a local strongman and buy land near him for protection. The kind of advice that makes you question every decision that led you there. But we weren't about to let our farm become just another cautionary tale. This was our land, our journey, our gamble. Our farm, our fight.

So, we dug in our heels and clung stubbornly to our 'hobie horse', which, by this point, had galloped well past the borders of common sense. Determined to make it work, we asked ourselves, 'How bad could it really get?' As it turns out, bad enough to call for reinforcements—but also good enough to prove that persistence pays off.

Meanwhile, Suzann, ever the broker-whisperer, was relentlessly chasing down the 7/12 transfer like it was the last train out of a pandemic-ridden Mumbai. Every week brought a fresh, imaginative excuse for the delay: COVID-19 lockdown, the entire area quarantined, the registrar isolating, the computers malfunctioning, Mars retrograding—you name it, they tried it. Mahesh, our very own detective-cum-man of all parts, kept prodding us to move things along, suspicious that something was rotten in the state of Raigad. Weeks passed with nothing but creative excuses, so Mahesh finally suggested we call the registrar directly. Good call, Mahesh.

The registrar was unusually forthcoming. A local man had filed an objection to the transfer, claiming he'd paid a 'token amount' to the seller—money she had conveniently forgotten to return. And, surprise, surprise, Farm Fiend had his fingerprints all over it. Suzann, always the calm, collected negotiator (ha!), lost her shirt and gave the broker a verbal lashing for the ages. The poor guy probably considered switching careers after that. 'Not acceptable. Fix this now,' she barked, in the tone that could peel paint off walls.

To move things along, Suzann dangled the prospect of a second farm purchase, promising the broker a generous commission if he sorted out the mess. And just like that, gears began to turn. Nothing gets done faster than when a commission is on the line. The broker, probably sweating bullets, managed to convince Farm Fiend to halt work on the road—which, by this point, had extended several meters beyond our farm's entrance and was beginning to look like it had ambitions of its own. He even pried the excavator out of Farm Fiend's grasp and handed it to Sanjay, who finally got back to the actual task of clearing land.

The broker, now fully motivated by financial self-preservation, started calling Suzann every few days with updates on the transfer's progress, probably terrified of another verbal lashing.

A week later, and a small payout lighter, our names were finally on the prized 7/12 Utara. Cue the applause.

We also had our very own, ludicrously overpriced stretch of soil called a road. Sure, it had cost an arm, a leg and perhaps a few toes, but at least we could now drive straight to the farm instead of parking in the hamlet and trekking through the wilderness, lugging tools, saplings and seeds like hapless, ill-prepared Sherpas.

Sanjay, in his now-limited excavator time, had managed to clear enough land for us to get serious about planting. It was happening. We were about to become actual farmers.

4

Under the Umbar Tree

June 2021

If securing the Satbara was a battle of wits, then transforming the land into a functioning farm felt like a quest out of mythology. Our land—raw, wild and unapologetic—was less a blank canvas and more a Jackson Pollock painting that required heavy machinery to decipher.

Before the ink on the Satbara had even dried, we'd already poured enough funds into what we disparagingly referred to as the 'Fiend Highway', our gloriously overpriced access road. In hindsight, it was a financial folly of epic proportions. Picture a jagged, narrow dirt path winding through the wilderness, lined with rocks that jutted out at exactly the right angle to puncture tyres and potholes deep enough to swallow a small car.

Our adventures in roadbuilding were soon followed by yet another foray into clearing the land. The farm was a jungle, dense and wild. Nature seemed to have set up its own fortress, complete with snake-like vines twisted around branches and thorns with a vendetta against us. We hacked and slashed through the undergrowth, dodging spider webs and the occasional snake, feeling like stars of our own jungle expedition movie. Just as victory seemed within reach, Sanjay came to an abrupt halt.

'There it is,' he announced with the reverence of a Nat Geo narrator. 'An Umbar tree. Sacred. It must not be cut.' The words carried the weight of a prophecy. Local lore held that water was always near an Umbar tree and that cutting one down would curse the land for eternity.

As city folk who were already tiptoeing our way into this rural world, we didn't need to be told twice. The tree became our silent guardian, a reminder that we were merely guests here. Conveniently, one of the borewell spots identified by Mahesh's water diviner was right next to it—a stroke of luck that felt as if the land itself had granted us permission to proceed.

And then, as if the land was rewarding our respect for its mystical heritage, we stumbled upon a hidden treasure—an invisible orchard. Mango, guava, cashew and jambul trees grew wild and free, bearing fruit as if mocking our efforts at cultivation. It felt like nature was extending an olive branch—or, in this case, a cashew branch—offering us a glimpse of its abundance if we proved worthy.

With the Farm Fiend out of the picture—for now—Mahesh and Sanjay reappeared in our lives and resumed their posts as resident experts and reluctant babysitters. Together, we sat down to draw up a list of all the crops we wanted to plant.

Spoiler alert: it was a very long list. We started off fairly reasonably—rice, mango, cashew, a few vegetables and some spices. But then every time M&S returned from the nursery after placing an order, we had a fresh burst of inspiration. 'Oh! How about chikoo (sapota)?' 'Tamarind! We must plant tamarind!' 'Bananas! Let's add bananas!' At some point, we had so many trees on the list that I think M&S considered relocating to escape us. Mangoes, cashews, guavas, chikoos, tamarind, neem, drumsticks, bananas, pepper, rice—we wanted them all, and we wanted them now.

And with a land-use plan as ambitious as our shopping list, we divided the farm accordingly. Nearly three-quarters of the slopes were reserved for mango, cashew, chikoo and banana trees—our future orchard in the making. The flatter sections became our experimental plots, where we planned, at some stage, to try our hand at sweet corn, peanuts, millets, wheat and, of course, rice. Some of it made perfect sense. Some of it didn't. All of it was exciting.

As the monsoon loomed on the horizon, the ticking clock grew deafening. To make the most of the rains, we had to act fast—planting was crucial, but drilling borewells was even more urgent. In this part of the world, borewells are almost always dug in May—that narrow, blistering window just before the monsoon arrives. By then, the water table has dropped to its lowest point after months of dry weather, giving you a clear sense of what lies beneath. If you find water in May, chances are it'll last you through the year. Wait any longer, and the rains might swell the cracks and crevices just enough to give you false hope. So May it is—dry, demanding and strangely dependable. However, in 2021, the usual urgency took on a sharper edge. Cyclone Tauktae had already ripped through Raigad, leaving the district looking like the set of a post-apocalyptic film: flash floods had gutted fields, ancient trees lay strewn like snapped matchsticks, and the highways were cratered and crumbling, more moonscape than road. Adding to the chaos, the monsoon was predicted to arrive early, cutting our timeline even shorter. Every farmer and landowner in the region was scrambling with the same idea, and borewell contractors—who suddenly seemed like creatures that existed only in rumours—were fully booked. Our calls were met with vague promises, evasive assurances and an infuriating reluctance to commit. Each day stretched on, heavy with the knowledge that the rains could arrive at any moment, potentially washing away our chance to secure water for our fields.

By 1 June, once Mahesh's ear had been thoroughly chewed and my nails worn down to nubs, we finally found a contractor willing to take on the job. Our hope took shape in the form of a massive boring rig—a relic of industrial might with a towering derrick and clanging metal arms—that emitted a relentless, grinding hum as it prepared to slice through the stubborn earth. Triumph—or so we thought.

That is, until the contractor arrived, took one look at Fiend Highway, and burst out laughing. 'Impossible,' he declared, his voice heavy with finality, as if we'd asked him to drive his rig across the Himalayas. The road was too narrow, too rocky and simply too ... fiendish. Our hard-won access road had turned traitor.

Panic set in like a creeping fog. We paced, argued and brainstormed, the hum of impending failure growing louder with every passing minute. Just when it felt like we were doomed to watch the monsoon arrive with no borewells in place, Mahesh had a stroke of brilliance. 'Let's ask the neighbour if we can use his land as a detour,' he suggested as if this were the simplest thing in the world. A few breathless negotiations later—peppered with promises, apologies and assurances that we were not, in fact, out to destroy his land—we had our detour approved.

But, as fate would have it, the drilling truck had other plans. It clattered its way through the makeshift path and promptly knocked down a section of our neighbour's carefully built fence, flattening a concrete structure whose purpose was unclear but whose importance was not. What followed was a flurry of phone calls, explanations and apologies. When a giant truck takes out a fence, there is no pretending it didn't happen.

Only after extended negotiations and repeated reassurances did the truck finally move forward. By then, we had aged a decade, but the borewell was at last within reach.

Drilling began after 10 p.m., with Mahesh sending us steady updates that read like reports from a long night's watch. Then came the unexpected good news. We struck water at just 50 feet in both spots, an extraordinary stroke of luck in a region where farmers often drill 300 or even 500 feet without success. With the borewells sealed and water waiting below, we chose to postpone the question of electricity for another day. For now, we allowed ourselves a rare moment of relief. It was a small victory, but one that mattered.

With our confidence soaring—and perhaps a touch of hubris—we did what any overly ambitious first-time farmers might do: we bought more land. This new plot lay seven kilometres away in Mahure, tucked so deep into the countryside that it felt like stepping into another century. No mobile network, no electricity, no neighbours—just wilderness stretching in every direction, unhurried and untouched.

The land exuded a quiet, untamed beauty, with wildflowers swaying in the breeze, a bubbling brook and ancient trees casting long shadows over rocky outcrops. We felt like we had stumbled into a forgotten Eden, a place where the modern world hadn't dared intrude. The stillness was mesmerising, almost meditative, broken only by the occasional rustle of unseen creatures in the underbrush.

In a burst of enthusiasm, we fenced it off—a symbolic claim on this rugged paradise—and promptly decided to let 'future us' figure out what to do with it. For now, it stood as a wild, untamed promise of possibilities, waiting patiently for the day we'd return with a plan.

Meanwhile, back on our farm in Mahagaon, Sanjay was quietly performing miracles. By the time we returned, he had dug holes for every sapling, fertilised the fields and prepared the land so thoroughly it looked as though planting could start the very next day.

Not a weed was out of place, and the farm, which had once looked like a wild tangle of untamed greenery, was now beginning to resemble something that might one day yield a harvest.

He'd even found help—Maruti, an enthusiastic lad from the nearby Adivasi hamlet, who became our first full-time employee. Wiry and energetic, he had an uncanny ability to appear just when needed, as if summoned by the sheer thought of work. He moved so quickly, darting between tasks with sprightly agility, that we nicknamed him 'the Imp'. There was a spring in his step, a mischievous glint in his eye, and a boundless energy that made him indispensable from the moment he arrived. Nothing fazed him—not the sun, not the dust, not even our chaotic to-do lists. He zipped through chores with the glee of someone who'd just discovered work was a competitive sport, and somehow managed to make even the most backbreaking jobs look like child's play. By the time we'd finished discussing a plan, he'd have already begun executing it, usually with some minor but eccentric modification of his own.

One moment, he'd be hoisting a sack of manure over his shoulder as if it weighed nothing; the next, he'd be circling a tree with the concentration of a fruit inspector, squinting up at the branches but making no move to climb it. We only discovered his fear of heights when he cheerfully sent his wife Vandana shimmying up the tree instead, while he stood guard below, offering advice and holding her slippers like a man fulfilling a sacred duty.

If a tool was missing, Maruti would produce it before anyone had a chance to look. If we were struggling with a task, he'd already be halfway through it, flashing his trademark grin as if the whole thing were a part of a long-running joke only he understood. Despite having no formal farming experience, he took to the work instinctively, adapting to each new challenge as though the skills had been lying dormant all along, just waiting for the right moment (and perhaps the right audience) to surface.

He had a particular knack for making the mundane oddly entertaining. Watering plants wasn't exciting enough, so he poked holes into an empty plastic bottle and turned it into a homemade sprinkler, twirling it through the fields and soaking everyone in his path. Keeping birds away from the crops morphed into a kind of rural performance art, involving a mix of theatrical whistling, wild arm flailing and, memorably, a spontaneous war dance that sent a flock of thieving parrots fleeing in panic.

Whatever the need—carrying, dragging, fetching, chasing—Maruti threw himself into it with a childlike glee that made the farm feel less like work and more like some beautifully choreographed farce. And somehow, that suited us just fine.

Soon enough, Vandana began accompanying Maruti to the farm every day—helping, chiding, guiding and very much pulling her weight. All thirty-five kilos of it. She had a sharp eye, a sharper tongue and a way of making people feel as if they were being watched—even when her back was turned. She didn't speak to us much, usually communicating through Maruti, but her silences carried weight. A quiet word here, a pointed glare at Maruti when he forgot to pass on something she'd said, and the message would land exactly as intended.

The only thing she asked for directly was a bluetooth speaker. After that, she could often be seen walking across the fields with it tucked under one arm, swaying slightly to her favourite Marathi songs—part scarecrow, part DJ and entirely in her element.

We were never quite sure whether she genuinely enjoyed farm work or simply preferred it to the responsibilities awaiting her back at home: three rambunctious kids, a mountain of housework and a household that never seemed to stop needing something. The farm, chaotic as it was, may have felt like a rare slice of control—or, at the very least, a change of scene.

Whatever her reasons, her dedication was clear. She showed up every day without fail, worked with quiet efficiency, and made herself indispensable without ever announcing it. Without being asked, she quietly took charge of hiring labour whenever we needed extra hands. And before we knew it, her parents, sisters-in-law and assorted extended family had become part of our daily workforce—as if she'd been building an empire under our noses, one relative at a time.

We made it official soon enough: Vandana was hired on a monthly salary, becoming our full-time employee number two—and the only woman in the hamlet with a steady job. Not that she mentioned it. She didn't need to.

And then came the biggest surprise of all: my husband, Sunil.

In the beginning, he had regarded the farm as a harmless hobby—something Suzann and I could dabble in while he continued his urban existence uninterrupted. For him, it was mostly a weekend outing: a scenic drive, a chance to stretch his legs, test the brakes, critique the state of rural roads, count how many potholes qualified as small lakes, enjoy the local Raigad speciality lapeta chicken, and then flee back to the promise of reliable Wi-Fi and air-conditioning that didn't require prayer.

But something shifted. Slowly, the farm began to pull him in—not just as our reluctant chauffeur or designated Marathi translator, but as a man who was starting to care. Before we knew it, he was pacing the land with a furrowed brow, making pointed observations about drainage gradients and diagnosing the terrain's inefficiencies.

'I'll help with logistics,' he had declared early on, in the manner of someone who had no intention of getting his hands dirty.

But the farm had other plans.

First, it appealed to his engineering mind: 'This land is wildly inefficient,' he muttered one day, shaking his head at the fields. 'How can there be no proper slope for drainage?'

Then, it seduced him with technology: 'You know,' he mused one afternoon, scanning the terrain critically, 'this whole organic farming thing could definitely use more tech.'

Just like that, Sunil anointed himself our resident tech visionary. To him, farming wasn't about nostalgia or rustic romanticism—it was an opportunity to transplant Silicon Valley into the soil. Precision mattered. Efficiency, he argued, wasn't at odds with sustainability; it was essential.

Before Suzann and I could fully absorb this shift, Sunil had us researching soil sensors, automated irrigation systems and composting methods that sounded suspiciously like lab experiments. He insisted on terracing the land—a project Suzann and I, with our romantic notions of keeping things wild and natural, would have endlessly postponed. But under Sunil's determined guidance, our land was quickly transformed into neat terraces designed to prevent erosion and optimise water retention.

His new-found enthusiasm did have one peculiar obsession: the excavator. This fascination remains baffling and slightly alarming. If he had his way, an excavator would be permanently stationed at the farm gate, ever-ready to respond to his whims to 'level this' and 'demolish that'.

'There's something deeply satisfying about watching an excavator work,' he sighed dreamily one evening, eyes fixed on the machine with the longing of a man seeing his childhood fantasies come alive. 'It's like civilisation in motion.'

Suzann and I exchanged concerned glances. Civilisation was great, but at Sunil's pace, our idyllic farm risked morphing into a construction site.

Yet, there was no denying the transformative impact of his relentless energy, modern perspective and, yes, even his inexplicable excavator fixation. For a city lawyer with zero previous interest in soil, pests or pipelines, Sunil was proving alarmingly effective as a tech-savvy farmer.

The following days were a whirlwind. Suzann, Sunil, Mahesh, Sanjay, Maruti, Vandana and I dove headfirst into digging, planting and sowing with joyful abandon. It was chaotic, muddy and exhausting, but also deeply fulfilling. Our friends, families, even Suzann's nephew and his friends joined in, turning the farm into an impromptu summer camp. The city kids, initially hesitant, soon embraced the mess with wild enthusiasm, running barefoot through the fields, rolling up their sleeves to pull weeds and flinging mud at each other with reckless delight. They arrived in clean clothes and ended the day looking like miniature farmers, their faces streaked with soil, their laughter ringing across the fields. There was something magical about watching them shed their city inhibitions and surrender to the simple joys of working with their hands. Seeing them dig into the earth without a care about getting dirty, their fingers muddy and their curiosity fully engaged, made the farm feel worth every obstacle, sleepless night and rupee we'd invested. There's a special kind of fulfilment that comes from watching people—especially children—connect with the land in a way that feels primal and pure, a reminder that the earth is meant to be touched, nurtured and understood.

So, if you're reading this and feel the itch to get your hands dirty, consider this an open invitation. Come join us on the farm. We never say no to free labour—especially if it's cheerful, messy and completely unqualified.

Getting out of your comfort zone is messy—trust me, I've had mud in places I didn't know existed—but it's worth it. There's a kind of peace in taking risks and sticking it out, even when it feels impossible. As Mahatma Gandhi so wisely said, 'To forget how to dig the earth and tend the soil is to forget ourselves.' And, to that I'd add—to dig the earth is to remember a part of yourself you didn't even know you'd lost.

5

Electric Poles

July 2021

WITH OUR BOREWELLS DRILLED AND SAPLINGS LOVINGLY planted, we stood on the verge of our next great challenge: electricity.

In the city, accessing electricity seems simple—you flip a switch and it's there. Out here, in rural Maharashtra, electricity felt more like a mythical creature: often spoken about, rarely seen and never reliable when you needed it the most. Without power for our submersible pumps, our saplings would wither under the sun faster than my patience does at government offices.

The nearest electric pole was just 300 metres away—a laughably short distance to our urban sensibilities. 'This should be easy!' I thought, with the blissful ignorance of someone who didn't yet know how far 300 rural metres could stretch in terms of effort, cost and sheer absurdity. Spoiler: very far.

In the days after we'd met Mahesh—and had promptly handed him a list of tasks long enough to make a lesser man run—he had introduced us, sometime in April, to his 'contact' at the Maharashtra State Electricity Distribution Company Limited (MSEDCL), the state electricity provider.

The man, a weathered figure with the wild-eyed intensity of a hobbit who'd been rudely dragged out of his cosy burrow into an epic misadventure, arrived at ten in the morning reeking of desi daru (illicit alcohol—moonshine to us folks). He paced our farm like a man on a mission, muttering cryptic phrases about pylons and volts as he gestured towards the horizon. At one point, he turned to us and said, 'Your power is there,' pointing to a distant electric tower with the gravitas of a prophet. 'Trust me. Give me your 7/12, and the current will flow before you can say cheers.'

We didn't trust him—besides, our names weren't even on the 7/12 yet—so we sent him on his way, feeling less like we'd secured electricity and more like we'd narrowly dodged a lightning bolt.

As we mulled over our dwindling options, the Farm Fiend made a theatrical return. If there were a local accolade for sowing chaos, he'd be its undisputed lifetime honoree. 'You'll need twelve poles,' he declared, his voice dripping with authority. Twelve poles. For 300 metres! Was he planning to power an intergalactic space station? When we baulked at the jaw-dropping costs, he leaned in and, dropping his voice to a hiss, said, 'Refuse, and your 7/12 may never see the light of day.'

His villainous monologue, delivered with the finesse of someone who had clearly practised before a mirror, achieved its desired effect—my stomach performed a tiny somersault. Yet, we stood our ground, though a lingering sense of foreboding warned us this wasn't the last we'd hear from him.

Months slipped by, and then the monsoon arrived, drenching our 400 saplings in a much-needed reprieve. We relied on that rainwater during the monsoon, but we knew it wouldn't last forever. Once the clouds dispersed, our focus would have to shift to tubewell water, which required robust pumps—and those pumps depended entirely on a steady supply of electricity. In our world, where every drop of water counted, ensuring a continuous power supply was not just important; it was absolutely critical.

In rural Maharashtra, electricity operates on an unusual and somewhat daunting principle: if the government can't extend it to your doorstep, you can bring it to yourself—for a price. The process involves paying to install poles from the nearest source, and for five years, these poles remain technically yours. During that time, anyone tapping into them owes you a fee. After the five-year mark, ownership reverts to the electricity board. It's a DIY infrastructure deal, which is as much about persistence as it is about power.

Finally, in July, M&S, our trusted farm scouts, introduced us to a third option: a new MSEDCL contractor—one who neither reeked of alcohol nor radiated malice. This man arrived at the farm with the quiet confidence of someone who got things done without drama. He paced methodically from the farm to the hamlet, measuring the distance with practised precision and marking out the spots for the poles. Finally, he turned to us and declared we needed six poles. Six! At last, someone who wasn't trying to fund their retirement at our expense. Relieved and buoyed by this glimmer of competence, we signed the papers, handed over the fees and allowed ourselves a fleeting moment of cautious optimism.

That optimism lasted exactly one week. The contractor called with grim news: the poles had arrived, but so had the villagers. A full-scale blockade awaited the contractor, complete with shouting, lathi-waving and accusations that we were there to steal their electricity. 'No poles, no wires, no current for outsiders!' they shouted, their voices rising in a cacophony of indignation. Reasoning with them felt like trying to explain algebra to a cat—futile and a little embarrassing for everyone involved.

A meeting with the hamlet elders was inevitable, and as fate would have it, both Suzann and Sunil developed pressing 'appointments' that day, leaving me to brave the storm alone. Well, almost alone—Kanan, my ever-intrepid sister, volunteered to accompany me, armed with courage and her smartphone, to document the drama (for posterity or perhaps a future Amazon Prime special).

On the drive over, M&S called with a last-minute suggestion: mithai diplomacy. Months earlier, we'd distributed boxes of sweets to the Police Patil and Lady Sarpanch as part of a charm offensive. Turns out, a well-timed box of mithai can do wonders and both officials were now willing to back us in our pole battle.

A bit of backstory. We first met the Police Patil at the broker's house when we signed our MOU. We dubbed him Farm Friend, clueless about what Police Patil even meant. Google enlightened us later. The Police Patil is a key figure in rural Maharashtra—a mix between a village elder, legal aide and the go-to person for anything semi-official.

Here's how it works: appointed by the state government, the Police Patil bridges the gap between villagers and the official police force. They handle various minor administrative tasks. Need a birth or death recorded? Call the Police Patil. Have a land dispute? He's your guy. They also help maintain peace and resolve minor conflicts, which makes them perfect for handling a standoff over electric poles!

The Police Patil is connected to the taluka magistrate and reports to the police department, giving him more influence than we'd realised. Lesson learnt: make friends with your Police Patil! Preferably with a box of sweets.

When we arrived, the scene was straight out of a spaghetti Western: villagers clustered in a tight circle, gesticulating wildly, their voices rising in a cacophony of grievances. Tobacco spit punctuated the air. My sister and I stepped into the fray, feeling both out of place and oddly resolute.

The meeting began with a surreal prelude—chatter about vaccines, politics and the pandemic. But as soon as the conversation veered towards the matter of our electric poles, the atmosphere shifted. The villagers' earlier wariness curdled into hostility. An older man, his face reddened with rage and spittle flying with every word, declared that we'd never get our poles. 'Not in a hundred years!' he spat, shaking a gnarled finger in our direction. Another villager muttered darkly about 'outsiders' ruining their peaceful lives, while a third launched into a completely unrelated tirade about a drunk city driver who had driven straight over a man sleeping in a corner of the hamlet.

As tensions rose to a boiling point, the Police Patil stepped in, calm and composed like a seasoned diplomat. He didn't dismiss their anger or mock their grievances. Instead, he listened intently, nodding at every wild accusation and murmuring neutral phrases of understanding. Slowly, with the patience of someone herding cats, he managed to steer the unruly conversation back to our modest request for six poles.

That's when the real objection surfaced. 'You're going to build a fancy farmhouse with air conditioners and steal all the electricity from our hamlet!' one man accused, his fluorescent orange shirt practically oscillating with the force of his indignation.

This was my moment. Summoning every ounce of sincerity, I stood up and addressed the gathering. 'No farmhouse! No air conditioners!' I declared, my voice trembling with sheer desperation. 'We just need electricity to run our submersible pumps.'

For a moment, the crowd froze. The man in the orange shirt paused mid-rant, his finger still raised, as if caught off guard. 'Pumps?' he repeated, his voice losing its edge, indignation slowly draining from his face. 'Yes, just pumps,' I replied, nodding earnestly, my heart pounding like a drum. Somehow, this simple word had pierced through the storm of accusations. And just like that, the tension melted away. The villagers, now reassured that we weren't here to disrupt their lives or steal their resources, exchanged murmurs of agreement. One by one, they began to drift off, their earlier hostility replaced by cautious acceptance.

Later, even as the last pole was planted and the wires finally connected, we held our breath. Then, with a satisfying roar, the pumps came to life—a sound so triumphant it could have been a symphony. Water burst from the borewells, rushing through the fields in gleaming streams. In that moment, months of frustration melted away, replaced by a surge of pure exhilaration.

Our 400 saplings, drooping under the punishing heat, seemed to spring back to life overnight. The parched earth softened, and the fields thrummed with new energy. That first surge of electricity wasn't just about running pumps; it was a hard-won victory over resistance, red tape and malice—a moment that proved we could make this dream work.

From that day on, the farm felt like a different place. The once-remote patch of land now buzzed with purpose—the hum of pumps, the growth of saplings (yes, if you listen hard enough, you can hear them grow) and the relief of no longer needing to lug water buckets like doomed characters in a rural epic. Electricity wasn't just power; it was progress with a capital P.

As we walked through the transformed fields, the rows of mango, cashew and banana saplings stood taller and prouder, a testament to everything we had fought for. The farm wasn't just a plot of land anymore—it was alive, brimming with promise and possibility.

The land, at least, had started to welcome us.

The neighbours, however, were another story.

6
Neighbours

August 2021–Present

IF THE LAND WAS SLOWLY WARMING TO US, THE HUMAN terrain proved far more complex. Our farm sat at the crossroads of three very different worlds. On one side were the Mumbai weekenders, drifting in with their curated countryside fantasies and their belief that rural life should come with Wi-Fi, mildly rustic decor and no actual discomfort. On another were the local farmers, steady and unsentimental, their days dictated by the sun, the soil and a no-nonsense acceptance of whatever the earth chose to give or take. And beyond them were the residents the Katkari hamlet, for whom time moved at its own pace and the forest always felt closer than the road.

And then there was us—two city dwellers who hadn't quite figured out where we fit in, and who the land, the local people and the general energy of the place hadn't fully decided about either.

Our nearest neighbour, a small-time politician from one of Mumbai's suburbs, was the embodiment of a very different kind of rural living. He had mastered the art of switching political allegiances as effortlessly as he switched between whiskey brands, always aligning himself with whoever was in power. His property, a sprawling six-acre estate, was proudly referred to as his 'pharmhouse'.

He was also the man we had approached, somewhat sheepishly, on the day our boring rig had refused to conquer Fiend Highway. After much theatrical sighing, several muttered lectures on rural boundary etiquette, and a display of posturing worthy of a village stage play, he had finally allowed us to drive the rig through a corner of his estate.

The rig had clipped a small section of his fence on its way through—and the price he quoted for that 'minor inconvenience' had been anything but small. It was our first introduction to the countryside's unwritten rules: every favour had a price.

Make no mistake, his 'pharmhouse' was less about 'pharming' and more about 'curated countryside luxury'. His mango grove was perfectly pruned, his tractor gleamed like a showroom model, and his solitary cow had the air of an animal raised on organic feed and daily affirmations.

Weekends at his estate were a spectacle—filled with hearty laughter, impromptu cricket matches and the clinking of glasses that drifted melodiously across the fields. From our scrappy corner of the land, we watched with a mix of awe and amusement.

One Sunday in August 2021, he strolled over, radiating charm and the unshakeable confidence of a man who had bent life effortlessly to his will. Casually, he suggested we buy his property.

For a fleeting moment, we considered it—not as a place to live, of course, but as a nearby retreat where we could catch our breath during long harvest days. That fantasy didn't survive the price tag. The amount he quoted was so astronomical that we half-expected the land to come with a private helipad and mango trees that harvested themselves.

Then came the clincher: of the six acres he was selling, only three were 'legally' his. The other three, he assured us with a wink, were 'borrowed' from the government. If we bought his land, he could get us a similar deal.

We politely declined, though not without marvelling at his audacity.

Shortly after his offer, his enthusiasm for the rural dream began to wane. His visits became infrequent, his once-manicured mango grove went wild, and the gleaming tractor vanished, presumably to a more deserving showroom. Today, his estate stands abandoned—a relic of a countryside fantasy that lost its charm once the novelty wore off.

Not far from his manicured 'pharmhouse', a very different kind of neighbour stood—or rather, slouched—in the form of a crumbling concrete structure that had once aspired to be a farmhouse. Its windows were chalked opaque with dust, vines curled lazily through the empty doorways and fractured beams invited thin columns of sunlight into rooms filled with silence. It had the unmistakable aura of a dream gone mouldy.

This forsaken structure belonged to a city-dweller whose brief foray into rural life had ended in scandal. He had been angrily referenced during my heated meeting about electric poles—a man whose attempt to integrate into village life had gone spectacularly wrong. According to local gossip, a drunken mishap in the hamlet had spiralled into a full-blown scandal, and rumour had it he was *strongly* advised to leave if he valued his life.

Following his hasty departure, the farmhouse was left to decay. At one point, his agent tried to sell it to us, enthusiastically describing it as a 'hidden gem with unlimited possibilities'. Suzann stepped inside, took one slow look around, and stepped right back out. 'It's a no,' she said simply, her internal vibe-meter—usually brutal but accurate—swinging hard into the red.

Beyond these abandoned ambitions, the land sloped gently upwards towards the Katkari hamlet. This was the hamlet that had given us Maruti the Imp, his wife Vandana, their three adorable children and, later, the extended families who would work on our farm. Life here was stark and resilient—no running water, no sewage system, no waste disposal. Just mud huts, woodsmoke, a handful of livestock and a way of living shaped by centuries of relying on the forest and on each other.

The families who lived there belonged to one of India's seventy-five Particularly Vulnerable Tribal Groups (PVTGs). Before the farm, I'd never even heard the name. Most of what I first learnt came not from conversations in the hamlet but from the internet—UPSC study notes, IAS summaries, PDF articles. There was something unsettling about that: how people who lived only a few steps away existed mostly as bullet points for exam preparations.

Katkaris live mainly in Raigad—our district—as well as in Palghar, Ratnagiri, Thane and parts of Gujarat. Traditionally, they were forest dwellers. Their name comes from 'kat', or catechu—an extract made by boiling the bark of the Khair tree. Once used as dye, medicine and food additive, it had sustained them for generations. The forest didn't just provide; it shaped who they were.

Today, many Katkari families are landless. Untethered from land, they migrate seasonally in search of work on farms, at brick kilns, construction sites—anywhere labour is needed. Their presence around our farm shifts with the seasons: some days women arrive with babies on their hips and sickles in hand; on others, children hover near the edges of our fields, giggling at our spinach or trailing behind labourers with shy curiosity.

Among themselves, they speak Katkari, a Marathi-Konkani dialect with its own soft, lilting rhythm. With outsiders, they switch to Marathi or Hindi. That quiet shift says a great deal: a hint of caution, a kind of practised self-protection.

They celebrate Undir Navmi, a festival devoted, without irony, to the rat. And once you've spent some time close to the forest, it starts to make sense. Nothing is insignificant out here; even a rodent has its place.

But not all of their history is theirs to embrace. Under the British Criminal Tribes Act of 1871, the Katkaris were branded 'habitually criminal', an entire community flattened into a stereotype. The act was repealed after Independence, but the stigma didn't vanish. It simply changed shape, visible in how neighbouring villages speak about them, in prejudices that surface during disputes, and in the slow, uneven access they still have to basic facilities.

I think about this sometimes when Katkari children wander past our fence, peeking into the toolshed or marvelling at the drip irrigation system as if it were a small miracle. They're wide-eyed, barefoot, full of questions. I wonder what they know of their history—of catechu and criminalisation, of forest livelihoods and forced labels. Maybe nothing. Maybe everything. Either way, the land remembers.

Scattered around the hamlet, stark against the mud and thatch, are half a dozen concrete toilet blocks—grey, angular, completely out of place. Built under the Swachh Bharat Mission, they were meant to signal progress. Instead, they stand abandoned, monuments to a plan made in places far away from here.

With no running water, no drainage, and no consultation with the community, the toilets were unusable from the start. Some now store bricks or hay. A few have become goat shelters, the goats wandering in and out as though they understand the irony better than anyone else. Others stand empty, their doors long gone, repurposed as firewood during winter nights. What remains are shells: cracked, dusty, stripped of purpose.

It's hard not to see them for what they are—another box ticked, another idea imposed without listening. Toilets without water. Concrete without context. As if building something, anything, counted as progress.

But our neighbours aren't amused. To them, these toilets are one more intrusion. One more reminder that decisions are made for them, not with them. And slowly, inevitably, that has bred something deeper than frustration—a quiet, simmering resentment towards anyone who comes from outside the hamlet.

And now we were part of that 'outside'.

Our early interactions with the hamlet were tense. Driving past felt like crossing a corridor of hard stares—silent, unblinking and heavy with history. No one had to say the words aloud; everything about their posture announced: 'you don't belong here'.

One afternoon in June 2021, all that bottled wariness boiled over. A group of men stormed into our farm, blocked our path and accused us of crushing a tin sheet while driving through the hamlet. When they marched Sunil back to inspect the damage, the sheet had magically appeared, crumpled with just the right amount of drama. He paid a few hundred rupees. Not a sum worth arguing about ... but more than enough to make us very, very wary.

And the tension didn't ease there.

What we saw as basic infrastructure, they saw as intrusion. The entire electricity saga—the blockade, the shouting, the accusations about ACs, the meeting under the blazing sun, the Police Patil mediating—has already been narrated earlier. But the memory of that day lingered like a stubborn aftertaste. To them, poles weren't progress; they were a threat. They were a reminder that outsiders arrived, changed things, and then left it to the locals to deal with the consequences.

Eventually, the poles were planted. The pumps roared to life. The saplings lived. But the distance between us and the hamlet remained—brittle, uneasy, hesitant.

And then, completely unexpectedly, something shifted.

It started with a frantic call from Maruti. A young girl in the hamlet was gravely ill and needed an injection costing around ₹15,000—something involving blood or platelets; I understood only the repeated words rakt and safed, and the urgency in his voice. She had been taken to a hospital in Indapur. It was a matter of life and death. Her family simply could not pay.

Maruti, trying to soften the weight of the request, added that her father would work at our farm at a reduced rate until the amount was repaid. But the child couldn't wait.

Of course we paid. And thankfully, she recovered.

The father worked at the farm for a few days and then slipped quietly back into the routines of his own life. The crisis passed.

But from that moment onwards, something subtle and significant began to change.

The stares weren't as hard.

The greetings weren't as forced.

We weren't just outsiders anymore—we had shown up at a moment that mattered.

Trust didn't arrive all at once. It seeped in slowly, through small, practical acts. We kept ORS—Electral—at the farm, a simple rehydration mix that, in these parts, could mean the difference between quick recovery and real trouble. Summer heat and post-monsoon stomach bugs had a way of knocking people out quickly, and Electral helped steady things before they spiralled out of control.

Our supply of cool, potable water became another source of quiet support. Buckets would be filled, bottles topped up and no one who came asking ever left empty-handed. (Yes, we've had the water tested; if this whole farming experiment goes belly-up, we may pivot to launching our very own artisanal mountain-water brand.)

Word travelled the way it always does in small villages—casually, efficiently. Before long, people from nearby hamlets began dropping in: some for Electral, some for drinking water and some simply because they knew help was available. And somewhere in the middle of these small exchanges, trust took root.

As that trust grew, so did our sense of responsibility. In the years that followed, when we finally had produce we could actually sell, we quietly set aside some of the proceeds for the children—to buy jackets, basic essentials and, on festival days, jalebis that created a happiness far larger than the treat warranted. Soon, even friends and family found their way into this circle—sending raincoats for the monsoon, warm clothes for winter, books and toys for the hamlet school.

Over time, this became a rhythm of its own. We began using our small earnings to buy exercise books, pencils, colouring books, crayons and all the school supplies that had somehow never reached the hamlet before. By our second year on the farm, the start of the school term came with a familiar ritual: the solitary schoolteacher would hand Maruti a handwritten 'wish list' for the children—a few dozen notebooks, some crayons, a bundle of pencils, maybe a chart paper or two. Their needs were so small, almost embarrassingly so, yet so essential. Why didn't the children already have notebooks? Why did the teacher have to rely on chance generosity to fill the most basic gaps?

We didn't have answers. All we could do was show up where the system hadn't.

In the winter of 2021, when the cold crept down from the hills, we bought monkey caps for all the little ones, their eyes peeking out from behind the wool like curious owlets. The following summer, when the sun turned ferocious, we brought hats to shield their heads as they dashed around the hamlet with the kind of energy only children possess.

And the happiest moment by far? Holi 2023, when we brought organic colours and water pistols for all the kids, and the hamlet turned into a rainbow stampede that left us unrecognisable and ridiculously happy.

It wasn't much. But it mattered—to them, yes, and quietly, unexpectedly, to us as well.

And with time, the responses shifted. What had begun as cautious nods, tentative waves and children peeking from behind a mother's saree slowly softened into smiles, then chatter, then warmth.

And finally, the children claimed us. Their unabashed waving, delighted giggles, and the joyful cry of 'Madam!' as we passed chipped away at a barrier that once felt immovable.

In the end, trust wasn't built through grand promises or big gestures. It grew out of tiny, steady acts—one ORS packet, one jacket, one shared moment at a time.

As our first winter settled in, marking the end of our very first year on the farm, we realised that the tension of those chaotic early months had dissolved almost without our noticing. The stares had softened, the waves had grown warmer, and we had found ourselves on firmer footing with the hamlet. For the first time, it felt like the farm—and the people around it—were beginning to let us in.

7

Still Standing: Year One on the Farm

If a tree falls on your farm and no one's there to hear it, trust me—it doesn't just make a sound, it crashes into your day, upends your plans and leaves you standing in the aftermath, wondering why you thought farming was a good idea. Farming has its own brand of philosophy, but it's the kind that doesn't come from books. It comes from mud-caked boots, aching backs and enough 'what-are-we-doing' moments to fill a memoir.

This past year has been a dizzying cocktail of triumphs, blunders and the kind of misadventures that could fill an entire season of *Khatron ke Khiladi: Farm Edition.* Suzann and I, despite our city-slicker roots and occasional cluelessness, have never once regretted buying this land. People call us 'terribly brave', but we know that's just code for 'completely mad'. And honestly? They're not wrong.

And so, this chapter gathers the stories from our first year that didn't demand entire chapters of their own—small victories, minor disasters and everything in between that still shaped the way we farm today.

Farming is a test of patience, grit and optimism—the kind that borders on delusion. But as we've learnt, sometimes stubborn optimism is enough to keep you going. From knee-deep compost pits to debates about mutant doodhis (bottle gourds), this year has been a masterclass in chaos. So, as we stumbled towards our first anniversary as organic farmers, it felt like the perfect time to pause, stretch our aching backs and reflect on everything we'd grown, broken, rescued and survived.

The Monsoon Chronicles

When the monsoon arrived, in July 2021, it didn't tiptoe in like a refreshing drizzle—it barged in like an uninvited wedding guest, loudly announcing its presence and proceeding to wreak havoc. Our so-called 'highway', which on a good day was just an ambitious dirt track, now resembled a lunar landscape—if the moon had been repeatedly bombarded by meteorites the size of buffaloes. Driving became an exercise in faith, physics and low-key prayer. We weren't so much steering as surrendering to the elements, bouncing over craters so deep they had their own microclimates. The car, our ever-loyal companion, groaned in protest, its suspension composing an opera of despair as we rattled our way towards the farm, wondering if we'd need a tow truck or a rescue mission.

But while the rain seemed intent on demolishing our roads and nerves, it turned the farm into an overachiever's paradise. Everything that had been planted with cautious optimism exploded into greenery, as if someone had cast a particularly enthusiastic spell. Patrel (colocasia) leaves the size of family-sized umbrellas popped up overnight, glistening like freshly waxed car hoods. Pumpkins, which had once been tiny and well-mannered, transformed into toddler-sized behemoths lurking under vines, looking like they might roll off on their own adventures. And the doodhis (bottle gourds)—dear lord, the doodhis—grew so fast we suspected they had ambitions of breaking world records. You could practically hear them stretching, an eerie vegetal creaking in the dead of night.

The bhindi (okra) and cucumbers also seemed to have developed personalities. The bhindi stood tall and proud, as if posing for a yearbook photo, while the cucumbers flailed around like excited game show contestants. Every visit to the farm became a lucky dip of surprises—what had grown, what had gone rogue and whether any of it would fit in our already overloaded car.

The drive back to Mumbai was nothing short of a pilgrimage, with our car transformed into a vegetable ark. Baskets of pumpkins, cucumbers and cartoonishly large doodhis were stacked so precariously that we resembled a slow-moving vegetable stall on wheels. Sunil drove with the precision of a surgeon and the reflexes of a rally driver—an unlikely but necessary combination for rural Maharashtra's roads. Suzann held on to a basket that threatened to escape, and I grumbled about the weight distribution. By the time we reached home, we would be covered in mud, slightly delirious and deeply satisfied.

Because it wasn't just produce we carried—we also carried proof that, despite the madness, the flooding and the car's traumatised suspension, we were *still* making this farming thing work. And that is how our farm became a Bollywood set—packed with action, drama and the occasional plot twist in the form of a giant runaway pumpkin.

Black Rice and the Sweet Taste of Vindication

In those first few months after we bought the farm in March 2021, we were still stumbling around like toddlers learning to walk—digging borewells, wrestling with electricity permissions that felt like a cosmic joke, and coaxing our first saplings into the ground. When the rains came, preparing our fields for paddy had been nowhere on the cards. But, as is the way in these parts, a man from the hamlet had been planting paddy in one corner of our land for as long as he could remember. When he realised we wouldn't be ready for farming that year, he asked if he could continue the tradition and even sweetened the offer by handing us a tiny portion of our own field on which we could try growing rice ourselves. He promised to sow it, tend it and even harvest it, if we just let him use the land for that season.

That little patch became our tiny gateway into rice cultivation. And once he'd drawn neat boundaries for where *our* rice would go, we did the most predictable thing imaginable: we decided to experiment. Why plant something sensible when we could try something wildly impractical? Enter: black rice.

Up until then, we hadn't really experimented with anything bold; we were mostly just learning how not to embarrass ourselves. Which is why the moment we got our little rice patch, we naturally veered straight into eccentric territory. Our black rice experiment was our first proper 'what's the worst that could happen?' moment—a tiny act of rebellion against Mahesh and Sanjay, our ever-sceptical farm consultants. They smirked when we handed the man a tiny sack of black rice seeds, their faces wearing that familiar expression reserved for city folk and their eccentric ideas.

But come September, the sweet scent of vindication drifted across the field. Our patch of black rice—dark, fragrant and unapologetically thriving—stood tall, its slender stalks swaying like they were marching in their own victory parade. The smirks faded. Mahesh and Sanjay muttered something that sounded suspiciously like approval.

And the harvest? An unadulterated triumph. We produced just enough for a single, sacred pot of kheer—rich, nutty and faintly floral—and every spoonful tasted like victory. Even the man from the hamlet, who had grown paddy all his life, gave us a quiet nod. It may have been the smallest harvest in Raigad district, but to us, it was a win worth savouring grain by tiny, triumphant grain.

The Not-So-Romantic Art of Sapling Babysitting

Watering over 400 saplings may sound like one of those picturesque farming tasks—the kind that city folk envision when they dream of returning to nature. In reality, it was less an idyllic toil under the sun and more a daily struggle of one man against a stubborn hosepipe and an army of perpetually thirsty trees.

Our mangoes, cashews, bananas and a few other hopeful recruits made their demands clear: survival was strictly conditional, and hydration was non-negotiable. Farming, we quickly realised, wasn't about planting and watching things grow—it was about relentless, back-breaking babysitting. And while *we* contributed moral support (and the odd appearance of usefulness), it was Maruti who did the real work—nimble, tireless and almost worryingly enthusiastic as he hauled the hose from sapling to sapling in an endless circuit.

Every morning, he set out like a one-man fire brigade, armed with sheer determination and a hose that seemed to have a personal vendetta. If the water pressure wasn't too weak, it was too strong, transforming the hose into an impromptu power washer that uprooted innocent seedlings. If the hose wasn't tangled around a tree, it was forming elaborate knots in and of itself, as if auditioning for a Boy Scouts handbook. By midday, Maruti's sweat dripped as freely as the water, and even his boundless energy began to wilt.

Enter Grim Sanjay, ever the voice of unsentimental wisdom. 'Drip irrigation,' he pronounced, a guru unveiling the secret to salvation. After recovering from the sticker shock of a few professional quotes, we decided to go the DIY route—where the Y, of course, stood for Grim Sanjay. After several days of pipe-laying, emitter-placing and heated debates that could have qualified as a minor engineering summit, we had a system so efficient that it felt like we'd unlocked black magic.

With water now reaching the roots where it mattered, the change was almost magical. The saplings shed their wilted, houseplant gloom, their leaves grew glossier, and they finally stood like trees that believed in tomorrow. Best of all, their grumbling caretaker was released from hose duty. Untethered, he channelled his energies into fresh mischief, while we, no longer driven by guilt, sat beneath a tree, listening to the quiet, contented hum of a farm finally doing what it was meant to do.

Of Tools, Toilets and Tiny Triumphs

With farming came tools—wheelbarrows, cutters, pumps and a collection of bits and bobs that seemed to multiply overnight, creeping into every available space like determined weeds. Maruti, being the unfortunate soul responsible for hauling this growing arsenal back to his hamlet each evening, was gradually becoming a human pack mule. Every night, he staggered off under the weight of shovels, pipes and mystery contraptions, looking less like a farmhand and more like a tragic figure from folklore—'the boy doomed to carry burdens until the end of time'. The eye-rolls and muttered grievances made it abundantly clear: we needed a solution, and we needed it fast.

But on a farm, even something as simple as a toolshed isn't just carpentry—it's diplomacy. In rural India, you cultivate relationships as deliberately as you cultivate soil. So when we finally decided to build a shed, we involved the sarpanch from the outset. It wasn't merely a courtesy; it was a quiet way of signalling goodwill, affirming that we were part of the community and ensuring that certain 'helpful' individuals—like the self-styled Farm Fiend—didn't take it upon themselves to 'manage' the project. Out here, every action ripples outwards; building alliances is as essential as building structures.

So we put up a toolshed to store our steadily growing collection of equipment, and a toilet, because while farming may teach patience and humility, some things simply cannot be postponed. Especially not when civilisation is a three-hour, pothole-riddled drive away, and the nearest alternative involves dense shrubbery and a suspiciously curious goat.

When it came to design, we flatly refused to go the way of the drab, soulless concrete boxes that dotted the countryside.

If we were going to build something, it had to *belong*. Enter chira stone—gorgeous, rustic laterite, rich with earthy hues that melted into the landscape. What emerged was not just a shed and a toilet but a pair of gingerbread-house-like structures so absurdly quaint that they seemed to have been plucked straight from a storybook. If we had topped them with icing instead of terracotta tiles, they would have been move-in ready for Hansel and Gretel, and maybe even a witch with a soft spot for aesthetics.

The toolshed stood sturdy and inviting, finally liberating Maruti from his nightly 'beast-of-burden' routine, while the toilet was nothing short of a revolution, bringing relief from desperate, last-minute dashes behind bushes.

In the grand scheme of farming, these were small victories. But to us, they were nothing short of Christmas miracles, delivering convenience, dignity and, at long last, a bit of order to our charmingly chaotic adventure.

A Masterclass in Humility (and Horticultural Rebellion)

Not all experiments were as rewarding. Unlike our monsoon bounty, our winter vegetable patch imparted a sobering lesson in humility. Spinach and coriander, ever the teacher's pets, behaved beautifully—growing in neat, disciplined rows, their bright green leaves rustling smugly in the breeze. Everything else, however, seemed to have entered some sort of a horticultural rebellion.

The tomatoes shrivelled in protest, rejecting both our care and our optimism. Carrots steadfastly refused to grow beyond tiny, stunted stubs that resembled toothpicks more than actual produce. And the brinjals—oh, the brinjals—suffered the worst fate of all. Their dark purple skins blistered under the merciless sun, casualties of an angry celestial magnifying glass. If vegetables had battle scars, ours wore their's proudly.

Enter the village experts, a chorus of self-appointed agricultural consultants who arrived whenever failure was in the air. They circled like detectives at a crime scene, offering conflicting verdicts with great authority. 'Too much sun,' one declared, shaking his head. 'Not enough water,' countered another. A third, not wanting to be left out, pointed gravely at the soil and proclaimed, 'Too rocky.' It became abundantly clear that farming was not merely about planting and watering—it was a game of chess where the rules kept changing, the board was uneven, and half the pieces kept disappearing.

Still, we remained undeterred. If the farm was a laboratory, then we were its mad scientists—tinkering, testing and stubbornly trying again. From vegetables to grains, every failure was just another step towards something that might eventually work. Some days, I told myself that success was just around the corner. Other days, I suspected it was hiding under one of those mutant doodhis, lying in wait, ready to ambush us the moment we let our guard down.

Farming Against the Grain

In this part of Maharashtra, farming follows a rhythm as old as the land itself. The monsoon arrives, rice is planted, the fields turn lush and green and then, just as swiftly, the rains vanish, the harvest is gathered and the land slips into an eight-month slumber. With the soil lying cracked and parched, farmers start to scatter—some tend goats, others seek daily wage work in distant towns. It's an unchanging cycle, dictated by the elements, respected like an unspoken law.

And then there was *us*—blissfully ignorant of these traditions, stubbornly refusing to let our fields rest. While the surrounding landscape turned brittle and brown, our farm remained defiantly green, a small, year-round anomaly fed by borewells, submersible pumps and drip irrigation pipes that snaked through the land like an elaborate nervous system.

At one point, the hamlet schoolteacher arrived with a group of children, treating our farm like an interactive museum exhibit. 'Look, children, *vegetables!*' he announced with the flourish of an explorer unveiling a lost civilisation. The kids, more familiar with paddy fields than spinach leaves, peered at our crop like it belonged in a museum display. Their curiosity was sweet—but also telling. To them, this was as unfamiliar as a foreign language.

That moment cemented something we had begun to realise: despite being in the heart of agricultural country, *we* were the *only* ones for miles with a year-round farm. While others planted with the rains and let their fields rest once the season ended, we had built an irrigation system that kept the land alive through every season. In a place where farming paused for months, we may as well have landed a spaceship in the middle of the town square.

Yet, every pipe and pump was also a stark reminder of our privilege. For generations, farmers here had worked within the limits set by nature, coaxing life from unyielding soil with nothing but patience and back-breaking labour. Watching them do so much with so little was humbling. It made every success on our farm feel bittersweet, a quiet acknowledgement that, for all our efforts, we were playing the game with a very different set of rules.

Farming Under Observation: The Village Elders' Watchful Eyes

Dedicating over an acre to vegetables? Sowing black rice? In this part of the world, such ideas were as outlandish as installing air-conditioning in a bullock cart. The hamlet elders, wizened men with years of monsoon wisdom etched into their faces, regarded us with a peculiar blend of fascination and concern. Their expressions hovered somewhere between admiration and suspicion, as though they were watching a particularly bewildering episode of an agricultural reality show—one they had never signed up for but now couldn't look away from.

It wasn't every day that outsiders willingly laboured in fields that weren't growing paddy, and certainly not people as hilariously unqualified as us. Their curiosity was evident in the way they lingered just a little longer at the edge of our farm, murmuring amongst themselves as they took in the spectacle—city folk, sunburnt and muddied, earnestly discussing soil pH and fungal spawn like we knew what we were doing. Some shook their heads, muttering about the absurdity of farming without simply surrendering to the monsoon cycle. Others watched with quiet amusement, as though indulging a particularly enthusiastic child attempting to build a house of cards in a wind tunnel.

Still, for all their scepticism, we caught glimpses of something else—an unspoken intrigue, a grudging respect, perhaps even a sliver of hope. Because, ridiculous as we may have looked, we were there, sweating under the same sun, battling the same soil, determined to carve out something new in that age-old landscape.

It wasn't just about crops—it was about convincing the land, the weather and, most of all, the people, that change wasn't always a bad thing. And for all the sweat, setbacks and eyebrow-raising experiments, we were proud of what we were building there. Even if it meant starring in Raigad's most bizarre unscripted drama.

By the end of our first year, the farm had turned into an unexpected teacher—one that didn't believe in theory, only in practical exams sprung on us without warning. We learnt through crises, through tiny triumphs and through the kind of daily improvisation that would've earned us honorary engineering degrees anywhere else. Nothing came gently: hoses snapped at the worst moments, saplings wilted for reasons known only to them, and every solution spawned three new problems. But in between those chaotic stretches were moments of pure, grounding joy—the steady unfurling of a leaf, the sudden burst of new growth, the quiet pride of watching something survive because we had tried a little harder.

When we began, we moved across the farm like tourists—curious, enthusiastic and mildly unsure of where the path actually led. But as the months passed, something subtle shifted. We found ourselves anticipating the rhythm of the land, adjusting to its moods, reading its silences. We no longer needed to ask what each patch looked like last week; we could tell. We no longer panicked at every droop or yellow leaf; we learnt to wait, to watch, to respond rather than react. The farm demanded patience, and somewhere along the way, we learnt to offer it.

The people around us seemed to sense the change too. The lingering glances from hamlet elders softened into nods that hovered somewhere between tolerance and genuine interest.

Maruti, overenthusiastic on his best days and unstoppable on the others, took ownership of the land with startling pride, patrolling it like a man whose name had been stitched into every corner. Even our toughest critics, Mahesh and Sanjay, started assessing our efforts with a little less scepticism and a little more respect, whether or not they admitted it.

But the real transformation was quieter. It happened in the way we showed up week after week, despite exhaustion, unpredictable weather and the kind of logistics that would have defeated saner people. It happened in the laughter that bubbled up even on the hardest days. It happened in the stubborn hope that refused to fade, even when the land pushed back.

It happened in us.

We stopped feeling like guests.

The land stopped feeling like an experiment.

And the farm—with all its contradictions, complications and comic timing—began to feel like ours.

A year on, the truth was simple: we were still standing. The farm was still standing. And, miraculously, so were a few of our trees. Which, in the great cosmic scale of farming accomplishments, felt like the perfect start.

YEAR TWO: 2022

8

A Popti Party

January 2022

YEAR TWO ANNOUNCED ITSELF WITH A SURPRISE: MAHESH, our manager, began exhibiting an unexpected new personality trait. The man who usually operated with the brisk efficiency of someone perpetually firefighting suddenly transformed into an eager host-in-the-making. Somewhere between supervising labourers and lecturing us about mulching, he discovered, much to his own delight, that he had a flair for event planning. One sunny afternoon in January 2022, he appeared before us with great ceremony and announced, 'We must throw a party to celebrate our farming triumphs!' I blinked. Triumphs? Did yanking out slightly fewer weeds now qualify as revolutionary agricultural progress? But Mahesh was undeterred, his fervour now bordering on evangelical. 'An evening party!' he declared, as though revealing the secret to eternal happiness.

My practical brain, already picturing the perils of navigating dark, twisting *un*roads at night, tried to apply reason. 'Mahesh, how about a lunch party instead?' I suggested, clinging to the faint hope of compromise.

'No way, madam!' he replied with conviction. 'Evening is when the magic happens!'

And just like that, it was decided. The date: Sunday, 6 February 2022. What lay ahead was a mystery, but one thing was certain—we were in for an adventure.

As the event drew closer, Suzann and I navigated the unknown waters of rural party planning with all the finesse of toddlers attempting a high-wire act. Panic began to creep in—not because of the scale of the event, but because neither of us had the faintest idea what to bring. Plates? Cutlery? Mosquito repellent? A fire extinguisher? Our sanity?

Just as I was about to enlist Sunil for one of his trademark acts of rural diplomacy, my phone buzzed with a message from Mahesh. It was clear, concise, and absolute: 'Bring biryani.'

Ah, biryani—the ultimate answer to every culinary dilemma. Suzann, ever the voice of reason, suggested moving the party to an earlier hour. But Mahesh, steadfast in his vision, squashed the idea like a fly on a fruit. 'No lunch! Only evening! People travel from miles around for a Popti Party!'

Wait, a *Popti Party?* We had no idea what that meant, but the wheels of fate—or rather, our car wheels—were now in motion.

We set off at 2:30 p.m., our car packed with a treasure trove of mutton biryani sealed under a layer of dough, nalli nihari, mithai and enough soft drinks to hydrate a battalion. For once, the traffic out of Mumbai was merciful, and we reached the farm as the golden light of dusk bathed the landscape in a warm, ethereal glow.

The surprises began almost immediately. First, there were no mosquitoes—an anomaly so miraculous it deserved its own celebration. Then, as if conjured by some benevolent farm genie, Maruti emerged triumphantly from the tool shed, hauling five mismatched chairs. He proudly declared that he'd secured them through a 'special deal' with his neighbours in the hamlet. The scene was completed by two large mats spread on the ground and an earthen choolah (clay stove) that looked straight out of an Indus Valley excavation site.

'Is that for the popti?' Suzann asked, her curiosity piqued.

'No, no!' Mahesh chuckled. 'That's for the biryani. The hay is for the popti!'

Hay? Our confusion thickened faster than the smoke that would soon engulf the cooking area. Before we could ask more questions, we found ourselves knee-deep in Popti (bhamburdi) leaves, freshly harvested from the farm. These leaves, which grow wild across Raigad in winter, are renowned for their medicinal properties. Maruti eagerly reminded us of the time he'd used these very leaves to stop the bleeding when Sunil had impaled himself on a thorn. 'Worked like a charm!' he bragged, as though he'd been a battlefield medic in a past life.

Even as he spoke, people from the hamlet began drifting into the farm. In ones and twos they arrived—kids and toddlers first, then older women with walking sticks, and finally the man in the bright orange shirt. They cackled and chattered, instantly turning the scene into a village-level production, either pitching in or issuing loud instructions on the 'correct' way to assemble a popti.

'We use these leaves to line the pot,' Mahesh explained, as if that alone decoded the entire recipe. The preparation of the popti turned out to be a spectacle in itself. Mahesh lined earthen pots with the Popti leaves before placing inside marinated chicken wrapped in banana leaves. Layers of beans, onions and potatoes followed, each treated with reverence. When the pots were finally sealed, Mahesh flipped them upside down, encased them in a mountain of hay, and lit the whole setup on fire.

Watching the flames eat through the hay was part thrilling, part terrifying. The fire roared to life with enthusiasm. The dry hay ignited instantly, crackling and hissing as it engulfed the pots, sending up thick plumes of smoke that curled into the night sky, a signal to distant farm deities. Sparks flew in all directions, making us question whether a fire extinguisher should have been part of our farm essentials.

At one point, the blaze leapt a little too enthusiastically towards the mats, causing a flurry of panicked stomping and frantic waving. 'All part of the experience!' Mahesh assured us, though his own eyes were wide with what looked suspiciously like second-hand fear.

The heat from the fire was intense, searing our faces as we stood mesmerised by the makeshift inferno. The hay smouldered, shrinking into glowing embers that radiated warmth into the crisp night air. As the fire died down, Mahesh expertly sifted through the ashes with a stick, checking the pots with the air of a seasoned alchemist evaluating his latest experiment, while murmurs of encouragement rose from the fast-growing crowd. 'Almost there,' he muttered, nudging the pots slightly before stepping back with a satisfied nod.

It was a high-stakes farm drama. Would the hay burn too quickly? Would the food survive this fiery ordeal? Would we?

The uncertainty made it all the more exhilarating. There was no precise science to it, just generations of intuition and the unshakeable belief that fire, if respected, would do its job.

And when the pots were finally pulled from the embers, their surfaces still warm to the touch, it was clear that the ritual had worked. The popti had cooked to perfection, infused with the smoky depth of the fire and the delicate fragrance of the leaves. As Mahesh cracked open the first pot, a billow of spice-laden steam curled into the cool night air, carrying with it the promise of something extraordinary.

Maruti let out an appreciative whistle. 'Now that,' he declared, 'is proper popti.'

No one disagreed. The fire had done its job, and miraculously, so had we. Forty-five minutes of suspense, careful tending and a few near-miss singed eyebrows had led to this moment. An intoxicating aroma spilled into the night, wrapping around us like an invisible embrace.

The experience was controlled chaos, equal parts culinary magic and borderline arson. Watching the pots emerge from their fiery burial was like witnessing a phoenix rise from the ashes—only this phoenix was stuffed with chicken and beans.

The chicken, tender and fragrant, surrendered to the slightest touch, slipping off the bone as if it had been waiting for this exact moment. The vegetables, caramelised to perfection, carried the deep, earthy sweetness that only fire and patience can create.

For a moment, no one spoke—words seemed unnecessary in the face of such an elemental triumph. Then, with quiet reverence, the first bite was taken. And just like that, the popti feast had truly begun.

As the evening wore on, we found ourselves laughing, eating and marvelling at how something so simple could feel so profound. The farm, in all its unpredictability, had gifted us yet another memory worth treasuring. On the drive back, dark and dotted with roadside stalls and buzzing wine shops, I found myself replaying the night in my head.

The Popti Party wasn't just about food—it was a celebration of resilience, a masterclass in embracing the unexpected, and an ode to the sheer absurdity of farm life. Farming has a mischievous way of tossing challenges like confetti, just to see how gracefully you'll dance through them. But every once in a while, amidst the chaos of water shortages, stubborn weeds and uninvited goats, it hands you an evening like this—one draped in laughter, laced with the scent of woodsmoke and filled with warmth from both fire and friendship.

Somewhere between dodging flying embers and debating whether Maruti had actually struck a 'special deal' for those chairs or simply 'borrowed' them indefinitely, we slipped into the moment completely. It was a night that didn't demand structure or meticulous planning; it simply asked us to show up, to revel in the unpredictability and to say yes to joy when life so generously offered it.

And so, as the last embers smouldered and the final bites of popti disappeared, we raised our mismatched cups in a toast—not just to the feast, but to the beautiful, hilarious and wildly unpredictable adventure of it all.

We didn't yet realise that the very ground beneath that celebration would soon become the subject of heated debate.

9

Boundary Lines and Other Myths

March 2022

AND ALMOST BEFORE THE SMOKE HAD CLEARED, THE NEXT chapter began.

Just as we were starting to find our footing, the ground beneath us became the centre of controversy—courtesy of the 'Great Government Land Survey'. What followed was an entirely new drama, complete with disgruntled neighbours, disputed boundaries and one particularly nosy goat who seemed far too invested in the proceedings.

The same goat from our very first farm visit trotted up as if checking on old friends, still looking mildly disappointed in our life choices.

Let's rewind to when we first 'saw' the land we were about to buy. Our broker, a man who possessed the theatrical flair of someone who might moonlight as a wedding emcee, gestured grandly as if unveiling a masterpiece in an art gallery. 'Your land stretches from that rock over there to ... um ... that bush yonder!' His sweeping arm movements made it look impressive, but my confidence waned when I realised this was a man who couldn't locate his own lunchbox without a GPS, let alone define our property boundaries.

At the time, the land was an unkempt tapestry of dry shrubs, towering trees and boulders, all tangled with enough scraggly bushes to resemble the set of a low-budget jungle movie. Against all logic, we bought it anyway, propelled by equal parts excitement and folly. And thus began our long, complicated journey trying to find out the exact whereabouts of our farm.

We were naïve but not completely stupid—we knew boundaries mattered. To avoid future disputes, we hired a private surveyor to mark out the edges of our newfound kingdom. Unfortunately, our neighbours, seasoned veterans in the gladiatorial sport of rural politics, immediately staged a revolt. 'We only accept the verdict of a government surveyor!' they declared, as though invoking a sacred decree. The private surveyor, sensing the shifting political winds, promptly packed up his equipment and left us to our fate.

Fine, we thought. Let's go official.

That, of course, was easier said than done. What followed was a bureaucratic odyssey of endless forms, notarised affidavits, identity proofs, property documents, NOCs from the village head (yes, really), and the infamous 7/12 extract—a document so omnipresent it haunted every step of our progress. To add insult to injury, surveys couldn't be conducted during the monsoon;

the relentless rains transformed the fields into impassable mud baths, making accurate measurements virtually impossible. This meant that for a full five months of the year, government surveys were off the table, and all the work had to be squeezed into the remaining seven months, inevitably creating a massive backlog.

Yet the biggest hurdle was the elusive government surveyor—a mythical figure whispered about, as slippery as a fish in a fast-moving stream. After months of fruitless phone calls and monsoon-soaked attempts to track him down, we finally cornered the man. His verdict: we were one of thirty pending surveys. 'Check back in nine months,' he said with the breezy indifference of someone handing out dentist appointments.

Meanwhile, our neighbours—completely unfazed by the concept of ownership—went about ploughing, sowing and eventually harvesting rice on land we were almost certain was ours. The audacity was as impressive as it was infuriating.

Finally, exactly one year to the day after we bought the land, the 'call' came. The government survey was scheduled for 17 March 2022. Notices were dispatched to all adjoining landowners, summoning them to witness the event. In my mind's eye, I pictured a medieval tribunal, complete with villagers armed with pitchforks, eagerly waiting to see if we would finally claim our rightful slice of the earth.

The day dawned bright and uncomfortably hot, the kind of weather that makes even birds go silent. We arrived at the farm with our friend Kanwaleen, who was visiting for the first time, and little did she know what kind of introduction awaited her.

The surveyor was already there, a man of brisk efficiency, equipped with what looked like relics from a Victorian scientific expedition: a tripod, a laser distance meter, oversized sheets of paper resting on an artist's easel and, most critically, a sack of powdered chalk. Maruti and his equally mischievous sidekicks were handed poles with reflective panels and dispatched to various 'corners' of the land. The surveyor then began his inscrutable work, peering through his laser finder, connecting dots on his paper, and occasionally muttering to himself while consulting what appeared to be a treasure map.

Land surveying, it turned out, was a dying art. Once the exclusive domain of men who braved jungles and mountains with little more than a theodolite and an iron will, it was now being replaced by drones and satellite mapping. The younger generation of surveyors was more likely to operate remote controls than stand knee-deep in thorny underbrush, marking out boundaries with chalk and twine. But here was a man from the old school, still doing it the way it had been done for centuries—walking the land, measuring it by hand and marking it out with nothing more than simple geometry, a steady eye and a well-placed line of powder.

Like a general commanding his troops, he barked out instructions, consulting his maps with the kind of focus one might expect from a man defusing a bomb rather than measuring a piece of farmland. Grim Sanjay, ever the sceptic, shadowed him like a suspicious detective, arms crossed, eyes narrowed, muttering the occasional dissent under his breath. Every time the surveyor adjusted his laser or marked a point with chalk, Sanjay would step forward, inspect it closely, and let out a quiet 'Hmm.'

The process was meticulous. The surveyor first identified an old government boundary marker—an inconspicuous stone buried half in the ground that, to the untrained eye, looked like just another rock. From there, he calculated distances, using his laser finder to locate the next point and cross-checking it with his weathered field map. Every time he confirmed a boundary, he marked it with a dramatic flourish of chalk powder.

He used an old-fashioned chain for measuring short distances and precise angles, stretching it across the land while mentally adjusting for slopes and undulations. 'Drones can't account for this,' he muttered at one point, kicking at a particularly deceptive incline. 'They think everything's flat. But land is never flat.'

Meanwhile, a crowd assembled, equal parts curious and sceptical. Some wandered into our vegetable patch, poking at the drip irrigation system as if it were alien technology. Others found their way into the tool shed, sprawling under the fan like weary travellers stumbling upon an oasis. And then there was the man with the goat—a small, black creature that followed him with dog-like devotion, as though questioning its place in the animal kingdom.

Then, right on cue, the Farm Fiend made his entrance.

He stormed onto the scene with all the subtlety of a Bollywood villain making his third-act comeback, his voice rising above the chatter. 'This surveyor has taken bribes to skew the boundaries in their favour!' he bellowed, eyes darting around for support.

The crowd, eager for entertainment, turned towards the commotion. Some nodded sagely, others squinted at the surveyor as though trying to detect the scent of corruption in the air. One man, caught between scepticism and the appeal of drama, muttered, '*Aaj kal sagle paise khaatat* ...' (These days, everyone takes bribes.)

The surveyor, who had clearly survived worse, barely looked up from his map. 'File an official complaint,' he said flatly.

The Fiend hesitated, weighing his options, then slunk away, leaving behind a trail of muttered threats. The goat, seemingly aware of the shift in mood, let out a long, tragic bleat, as if lamenting the lost potential for chaos.

With that, the survey continued, uninterrupted. After hours of precise measurements, chalk lines and animated disputes over a particularly ambiguous tree, the surveyor gathered five witnesses, secured their signatures and declared the task complete.

Without so much as a glance at the vada pav we'd offered in gratitude, he packed up his equipment and slung his tripod over his shoulder like a cowboy about to ride off into the sunset. His only request? Cold water. By sheer luck, Sunil had brought along an icebox packed to the brim with small water bottles. We handed one over, watching as he took a long, measured sip before nodding in approval. Then, without a word, he strode off, leaving us with freshly drawn boundary lines, a lingering sense of relief and an unexpected lesson in the art of quiet efficiency. Bless him!

And so, we finally had our boundaries defined. After twelve months of uncertainty, we knew, at long last, which trees were ours and which bushes marked the edges of our land.

With our boundaries finally set and the last of the vada pav devoured, we thought we could relax—at least for a day.

But on a farm, there's no such thing as downtime.

No sooner had we celebrated our small victory than the next challenge came charging—quite literally—through our fields.

10

The Bull Run

April 2022

WITH BOUNDARIES FINALLY DEFINED, GRIM SANJAY, OUR ever-dependable farm consultant, threw himself into fencing the property. Meanwhile, Maruti and his equally industrious wife began planting what could only be described as an agricultural buffet: tomatoes, chillies, brinjals, okra, sweet potatoes. If it could grow, they planted it. Within weeks, we were reaping spinach, fenugreek, coriander and marigolds in dazzling abundance. For a brief, fleeting moment, we dared to believe we were living the dream. A messy, muddy dream, but a dream nonetheless.

The trouble began with a phone call in mid-April 2022, the sort of call that never brought good news where the farm was concerned.

Mahesh's voice came through in rapid-fire Marathi, urgent enough to make my stomach drop. 'Ghure ni bhaji khalli!' he declared, breathless. My Marathi is functional at best, and 'ghure' was nowhere in my limited vocabulary. A person? A demon? Some local deity with a fondness for vegetables?

Before I could cycle through the entire Mahabharata of possibilities, Mahesh clarified: a herd of marauding cows had broken in and eaten everything.

And just like that, our farm had been ambushed.

By then, we should have been prepared for anything, but somehow every mishap still managed to blindside us just when we dared to think things were under control. It sounded like a cliché to say there was never a dull moment, but after fourteen months of navigating ornery land sellers, squabbling with power-hungry village elders and conducting water-boring operations deep into the night, it truly felt like the universe was watching us, grinning mischievously while rolling a pair of dice.

The next morning, we raced to the farm, bracing ourselves for disaster. What greeted us was a scene straight out of an agricultural apocalypse. The vegetable patch had been decimated. Okra stalks lay flattened, brinjal plants had been ripped out of the ground and even our sturdy banana, papaya and drumstick trees bore the scars of the bovine onslaught.

Oddly enough, the tomato plants had remained untouched.

Sanjay informed us that the smell of tomato leaves was a natural deterrent, even to cows with otherwise indiscriminate tastes. One could almost picture them sniffing disdainfully before moving on to demolish the rest of the feast.

Sunil let out a long breath, surveying the flattened okra and brinjal plants with the weariness of a man who had seen too much.

'You know,' he said, rubbing his temples, 'I always thought farming disasters would be more ... natural. You know, droughts, floods, maybe the occasional plague of locusts. Not this.' He gestured helplessly at the destruction. 'Not cows staging an overnight invasion like some kind of hoofed militia.'

Maruti, who had been brooding near the ruined vegetable patch, perked up. 'Madam, I can stay at the farm at night to keep watch!'

We all turned to look at him.

'You'd stay here, alone?' I asked sceptically.

'Yes! I will be like a—' he paused, searching for the right words. 'Like a *tiger*!'

There was a beat of silence.

Sunil raised an eyebrow. 'Maruti, you were terrified of a *chameleon* last week.'

Maruti cleared his throat. 'Yes, well ... this is different.'

Suzann patted his shoulder. 'Of course it is, Maruti. Let us know when you've perfected your roar.'

To lift spirits (and possibly distract ourselves from the carnage), we decided to plant a hundred new banana trees. It was equal parts practical and a little bit desperate, but planting felt like a way to reclaim the land from chaos. We spent the afternoon pacing the fields, planning where the trees would go, and marvelling at the resilience of the tomato patch—a small but meaningful victory in the face of disaster.

But the farm gods weren't done with us yet. Just days later, Mahesh called again, this time with a tone that bordered on disbelief.

'Are you sitting down?' he asked.

'That depends,' I said. 'Do I want to be?'

He sighed. 'Someone has stolen all the tomatoes.'

Once again, we raced to the farm the next morning to assess the damage.

Every last tomato was gone.

For a long moment, we just stood there, absorbing this latest absurdity.

Sunil exhaled slowly. 'This is it. This is the moment I give up and start believing in curses.'

Suzann folded her arms. 'We should just set up a sign at the gate: "Farm-fresh vegetables, free for anyone with hooves or a criminal record."'

I imagined the thief creeping stealthily through the rows, giggling maniacally as he loaded his bounty. Maybe he planned to have a tomato-based empire. Or maybe he just really loved tomato chutney.

'Well,' I said finally, 'at least someone appreciated our farming efforts.'

Suzann crossed her arms. 'I'd prefer appreciation in the form of money. *Not* grand theft tomato.'

Sunil shook his head. 'I don't even know what to be more upset about—the fact that our tomatoes got stolen or the fact that we didn't think to sell them first.'

Mahesh, watching our growing exasperation, tried to look reassuring. 'Don't worry, madam. I will ask around. We will find the culprit.'

I sighed. 'Mahesh, I don't think I have the energy to launch an investigation over stolen tomatoes.'

By that point, there was nothing left to do but pour all our energy into the one thing we could control: the fence. When it was finally completed, it stood tall and imposing, a fortress around our beleaguered farm. We even installed heavy iron gates with the sturdiest locks money could buy. If the cows wanted to stage a sequel, they would have to figure out how to operate a padlock first.

With the fence in place, we finally felt like we could breathe—at least until the next calamity arrived. Farming, it turned out, hadn't been about keeping things under control; it had been about learning to make peace with chaos.

A week later, as the sun dipped behind the hills, I walked the boundary of our newly fortified farm. The air was cool, the fields glowed gold, and the earth under my feet—stubborn, uneven, quietly alive—felt almost companionable. I crouched, let the soil slip through my fingers and realised, with a surprising, steady calm, that farming wasn't simply about growing things. It was about letting the land grow us too—one mishap, one triumph, one unexpected lesson at a time.

Soon enough, the next lesson arrived, and it involved mango trees rather than fences or cattle.

11

How to Train Your Mango

May 2022

THE EIGHT OLD MANGO TREES STOOD SCATTERED ACROSS our land like ancient sentinels—tall, gnarled and wholly unimpressed by our grand plans for a mango orchard. They had clearly survived decades of storms, attacks by grazing cattle and human neglect, and they looked at us (or so it felt) with the weary patience of elders humouring excitable children.

Grim Sanjay, our ever-pragmatic farm consultant, had taken one look at them during our very first walkthrough and delivered his verdict with absolute certainty. 'They're wild trees,' he'd said, tapping a trunk as though diagnosing a patient. 'They'll never fruit well on their own, but you can graft good varieties onto them.'

'Graft?' Suzann asked, narrowing her eyes. 'As in ... tree surgery?'

Sanjay gave her one of his trademark unimpressed looks. 'Not surgery. Just a small operation.'

'So ... surgery,' I muttered. He ignored me completely.

Still, we had understood the message. If these stubborn old trees weren't going to give us good fruit on their own, we would simply have to help them along. They weren't hopeless—not with trunks that solid, canopies that wide, and a root system that had clearly dug itself deep into the red soil long before we had ever arrived. And so began our initiation into the unexpectedly delicate world of mango transformation.

The thick canopies made it clear that these trees had potential. With the right intervention, they could be coaxed into bearing the kind of mangoes that people actually wanted to eat—the kind with sun-kissed golden skin, honeyed flesh and the sort of fragrance that screamed summer.

To make that happen, we would turn to grafting, an ancient horticultural technique that allows two different plants to merge into one. By attaching a cutting from a desirable fruiting variety onto a strong, established tree (called the rootstock), we could essentially trick the old tree into adopting the new branch as its own. If successful, the tree would abandon its original, unimpressive variety of fruit and instead produce the prized mangoes from the grafted variety. Think of it as an organ transplant—but for trees.

Enter the Graft Man, a well-built expert with the steady hands of a surgeon and the no-nonsense attitude of a man who had performed more tree operations than he could count. He arrived armed with an intimidating blade, a deeply ingrained scepticism about our farming credentials and a satchel of freshly cut scions—young branches taken from proven fruit-bearing mango trees, carefully selected for their ability to fuse with the old rootstock and produce high-quality fruit.

'You want all six varieties on all eight trees?' he asked, arching an eyebrow as he inspected our chosen specimens. 'Hmm. Ambitious.'

'Is that ambitious-good or ambitious-bad?' I asked, warily.

'That depends,' he said, shrugging. 'You willing to wait?'

We exchanged glances. Waiting wasn't our strongest suit, but farming had been breaking down our impatience one crop at a time.

'We're learning,' Suzann admitted.

That seemed to satisfy him. Without another word, he got to work, slicing into the old trunks with precision.

The process began with an act that felt almost sacrilegious. The towering wild mango trees were cut down to a mere five feet in height, and their branches ruthlessly pruned until all that remained was a stark, skeletal frame. The idea behind this aggressive pruning was simple but essential: by cutting away excess growth, we could ensure that the tree's nutrients and energy would be redirected towards the new grafts rather than into sustaining unnecessary foliage.

Once the trees had been reduced to their essential forms, the real magic began. The Graft Man worked swiftly, making precise cuts and securing the scions in place. Each graft was meticulously bound and protected, a delicate surgery that would determine whether our wild trees would transform into productive orchard trees.

Under his guidance, we grafted six different mango varieties—Alphonso, Dasheri, Vanraj, Payri, Kesar and Totapuri—onto all eight trees, turning each into a veritable mango medley.

We wrapped and secured each graft as if swaddling a newborn, whispering silent prayers to the gods of horticulture.

At first, nothing happened. Days turned into weeks, weeks into months. We monitored the grafts with the nervous energy of parents awaiting board exam results. And then, one miraculous morning, we spotted it—a delicate new shoot emerging from a scion. The graft had taken. It was alive!

Like proud farmers (or mildly obsessed plant stalkers), we hovered over our experimental trees, willing them to flourish. Soon, the scions began to sprout, their young leaves a hopeful green against the weathered bark of their host trees.

Sanjay, who had suggested grafting in the first place, inspected the growth with the satisfaction of a man who had, of course, been right all along. He gave a slow, approving nod. 'It'll work,' he admitted—his version of a standing ovation.

But we knew the real test was still ahead. The process demanded patience. The grafts had to be monitored closely, their union with the rootstock painstakingly checked for signs of acceptance or rejection.

There was something poetic, almost philosophical, about this entire transformation. Here were these old, resilient trees, their roots embedded deep in the history of this land, yet they were being asked to adapt, to embrace change. We, too, were in the process of transformation—city-dwellers attempting to shape ourselves into farmers, making mistakes, learning and hoping that, like our mango trees, we would eventually grow into something worthwhile.

As of this moment in our farming saga, the trees still haven't fruited, but the grafts are thriving—shoots thickening, leaves multiplying as if they know something we don't.

Until then, we wait and learn yet again that farming is mostly about faith, a lot of grafting tape, and the sheer audacity to believe we can outsmart a mango tree.

But patience isn't exactly Suzann's strong suit. While the mango trees took their time deciding whether to reward our efforts, she had already set her sights on a more immediate, high-reward venture. And thus, the Great Mushroom Mutiny began.

12

The Great Mushroom Mutiny

May 2022

OF ALL THE DREAMS WE HAD FOR OUR FARM—LUSH RICE paddies, endless tomato vines, orchards brimming with fruit—perhaps none was as bold, as groundbreaking or as 'audacious' as Suzann's vision for an oyster mushroom empire.

'Low effort, high return,' she declared one evening over drinks, waving a wine glass like a general surveying a battlefield. 'Restaurants will *fight* over my mushrooms. We'll be pioneers.'

Initially, I thought it was just another one of her whimsical ideas—like the time she suggested growing avocados in our rocky, stubborn soil, blissfully ignoring the minor inconvenience of 'climate unsuitability'. But after some rocky negotiations (pun intended), we found a patch of land that seemed perfect for mushroom-growing.

Maruti and his crew swiftly built a dark, snug shed—a simple wooden frame with a hay-thatched roof, designed to provide the perfect, shaded environment for fungi to flourish and, as we would later discover, a bit *too* inviting for curious critters.

The first batch of mushroom bags were treated like royalty. They were carefully prepped, lovingly suspended from bamboo racks and misted with the delicate touch of a first-time parent adjusting a newborn's swaddle. Suzann hovered over them like a doting mother, whispering words of encouragement.

'Grow, my babies,' she murmured, inspecting the faint white tendrils of mycelium spreading across the substrate.

Sunil, ever the sceptic, raised an eyebrow. 'Should we be concerned that she's talking to fungi?'

'Let her have this,' I said. 'We need a win.'

A sheet of blue tarpaulin was laid on the ground, and a single low-voltage bulb illuminated the shed, because mushrooms like it dark and warm. The entire set-up was reminiscent of a covert scientific experiment, or possibly an illegal brewing operation. Mahesh, our ever-willing farm manager, had done a crash course on mushroom cultivation to cater to our latest whimsy. He instructed Maruti on water misting schedules, the necessity of a sterile atmosphere and other fungal secrets.

When we visited, we had to remove our shoes and quickly slip in through the tarpaulin-wrapped door, lest our reckless intrusion expose the fungi to germs or sun shock. We weren't entirely sure what sun shock looked like, but we imagined traumatised mushrooms keeling over dramatically, their delicate spores screaming in protest.

After a brief bout of spore-related confusion (involving a misplaced bag and much finger-pointing), we managed to harvest our first batch of oyster mushrooms. To our delight, these little fungi turned out to be both ridiculously easy to grow and wildly in demand.

Before long, plump, pristine mushrooms began sprouting like overachievers at a school science fair, practically shouting, 'Market us at premium rates!' But, as was our wont, we hadn't exactly planned for a fungi growing schedule. Turns out, mushrooms don't care about *our* convenience. When they were ready, they had to be harvested *immediately* and rushed to a cool storage place for consumption within a few days.

We had over forty mushroom sacks, and all of them were eager to give us several kilos of mushrooms at an alarming frequency.

For a few weeks, we found ourselves charging off to the farm multiple times a week, armed with oversized ice boxes and a growing sense of panic. There was no escaping the oyster mushroom avalanche. We pressed mushrooms into the hands of friends, neighbours, unsuspecting visitors—anyone who so much as glanced in our direction.

Mushroom risotto, stir-fry, butter garlic mushrooms, mushroom curry, pea and mushroom sabji—we cooked them every which way, until the mere sight of those fleshy little caps induced despair.

After a couple of months, we calmed down enough to admit defeat. We instructed Mahesh to distribute the fungi to anyone in the hamlet or in his home at Indapur who knew what it was and was willing to consume it. Interestingly, the most eager oyster mushroom lover turned out to be the teacher in our local hamlet. Maruti and his kin, of course, flatly refused to try this odd-shaped thing that had dared to grow without sunlight.

And then the season changed. The monsoon arrived.

The first real downpour turned our charming little shed into something resembling a sinking ship. The thatched roof, which we had assumed would *repel* water, soaked it up instead—swelling like a sponge until droplets began to fall steadily onto the mushroom bags below. Soon, the interior wasn't just damp; it was a breeding ground for trouble.

Then came the mice.

It started subtly—a faint rustling in the corners, a few chewed strands of hay. Nothing to panic about. But one morning, as we stepped into the shed, Suzann let out a strangled gasp and pointed.

'WHAT. IS. THAT?'

We followed her trembling finger to the unmistakable little black pellets scattered across the bags.

'Mouse droppings,' Sunil confirmed grimly.

'No,' Suzann whispered, eyes wide with horror. 'No, no, no. My mushrooms are supposed to be organic, not *artisanal rat housing*!'

A quick investigation revealed that our precious mushroom bags had been turned into a full-fledged rodent resort. The mice—clever little opportunists—had discovered that our hay-thatched roof wasn't just a leaky mess, but also prime real estate for nesting. It was warm, sheltered and—thanks to the gentle humidity—shockingly hospitable for an entire colony of freeloaders.

The final straw came when we found a pair of tiny, beady eyes staring at us from inside one of the mushroom bags.

Suzann recoiled. '*Did that mouse just look at me like it owns the place?*'

'At this point, it *does*,' I said.

And so, with heavy hearts and a great deal of grumbling, we admitted defeat. The mushroom shed was officially condemned. The bags were discarded, the racks dismantled, and the rodents evicted (though I suspect they simply moved into the next closest structure).

'Well,' Sunil said, watching Suzann survey the ruins of her dream, 'that was short-lived.'

Suzann crossed her arms. 'I refuse to go down like this. This isn't over.'

But for now, it *was* over. If the mushroom dream was to rise again, it would require a permanent, rodent-proof structure—a real shed with 'walls', a proper roof and a mouse deterrent plan that didn't rely on optimism and denial. I glanced at Suzann. 'So ... should I still call you the Mushroom Queen?'

She sighed dramatically. 'No. The tiara is in storage. *For now.*'

As we drove away, leaving the leaky shed to the mice and their flourishing dynasty, one thing was clear: the land had gently—very gently—suggested that we stick to crops it actually approved of.

13

Kharif Planting

June 2022

Suzann's mushroom shed had barely settled into its new identity as a rodent hostel when the skies began to shift. By June 2022, the monsoon clouds rolled in, declaring that our days of delicate fungi were over. It was time for crops that actually belonged here—rice, millets, pulses—and for our first true kharif season.

The land was ready. Now we had to be.

Kharif, as we quickly learnt, is not just a growing cycle—it is a mood. A declaration. A phenomenon. When the first rains fall, farmers across India head to their fields with a kind of collective muscle memory honed over generations. Rice saplings emerge in neat green lines, the air thickens with the smell of wet earth,

This was the land we bought. Nothing like the idyllic brochure we had in our heads.

Walking the land for the first time. Listening more than planning.

Step one: bring in a JCB and optimism. Both wildly under-qualified for what lay ahead.

The Fiend Highway. A road we paid for, whether we were ready or not.

Planting the first trees: the moment we realised farming is mostly bending and sweating. I managed to get a tear in my rotator cuff; most painful and inconvenient. Clearly, we did not know what we were doing.

Rice cultivation, traditional edition. When technology gives way to bullocks and common sense.

Learning to transplant rice the old way: slow, muddy and under expert supervision. Finding the occasional crab and watching out for snakes.

The rhythm of the field. Bent backs, green bundle and a silence that teaches more than Google ever could.

The reward phase. When the farm stops looking theoretical and starts looking alive.

Two Bandra Girls, briefly convinced we know what we are doing.

Oversized gourds, improbably suspended. The farm finding its proportions.

Proof of concept. Also proof that vegetables have a sense of humour.

Infrastructure, farm-style. Local chira stone to build the basic necessities: a toolshed and a toilet. No frills.

Harvest, finally. Not pretty, not perfect and absolutely ours.

You eat what you can and can what you can't. Too many tomatoes to give away. Which is how sauce entered the story.

Somewhere along the way, it became a place that belonged to us all.

Mahure. Paradise, for now. The kind of quiet that makes us nervous. Keep the developers away.

Two Bandra Girls. Zero restraint. Oversized vegetables.

and every conversation begins and ends with predictions about the monsoon.

For us, however, this was uncharted territory.

Yes, we *had* grown a thimbleful of black rice the previous year, but if we were being honest, that didn't really count. All we had done was hand a tiny sack of seeds to the man from the hamlet who had been planting paddy on our land for decades. He had sowed it, tended it, harvested it and even humoured us with that celebratory pot of black-rice kheer. It was our rice in theory, his in practice.

But 2022 was different. This year, the paddy fields were ours to prepare. Ours to sow. Ours to coax through rain, wind, pests, tantrums and triumphs.

The real kharif season had arrived, and we were finally in the arena.

The first challenge was selecting land that could hold enough rainwater to sustain rice. Given our farm's location on the slopes of the Sahyadri mountain range, this was no small feat. The terrain was a chaotic mix of high and low ground, with dry rocky patches sitting awkwardly beside waterlogged depressions. Some areas drained too quickly; others were prone to turning into shallow lakes. The goal was to find about 1.5 acres of relatively level land that could hold moisture long enough for the rice to take root without drowning it entirely.

Grim Sanjay surveyed the land with a scowl, kicking at the occasional rock as if trying to intimidate it into moving. Sunil, never one to trust mere human instincts, pulled out an Altimeter app on his mobile that measured elevation and slope. The results were not encouraging—the app cheerfully informed us that our chosen patch was more suitable for skiing than farming. Meanwhile, Suzann and I wandered behind them, marking imaginary bunds in the soil with sticks, hoping that if we looked confident enough, the land would cooperate out of sheer politeness.

'This bit looks flat,' Suzann announced, driving a stick into the ground like an explorer claiming new territory.

'That's because we're standing on it,' I pointed out.

After much debate, rock-kicking and a reluctant acceptance of reality, we settled on three largish plots where water could naturally pool, plus a few smaller sections optimistically labelled 'experimental'. (Translation: places where things might drown, dry up or mysteriously disappear.) Maruti and his crew were dispatched to clear the land, hacking through the undergrowth, removing stubborn shrubs, and rolling aside smaller rocks even as boulders were grudgingly accepted as part of the landscape.

Next came the bunds—thick walls of packed mud, their edges stamped down by bare feet, forming raised barriers to hold water once the rains arrived. It was slow, messy work, and even with all hands on deck, the fields didn't yet resemble anything that could grow rice. What we needed now was someone who actually understood paddy.

That was when Mr Vishwas Pingle entered our story.

A seasoned rice farmer from a neighbouring village, Vishwas had been recommended to us with the kind of confidence usually reserved for men who can coax miracles out of mud. We contracted him to help us navigate our first real paddy season, and he arrived with the self-assured gait of someone who had spent his entire life ankle-deep in slush.

He was tobacco-chewing, sharp-eyed and cheerfully blunt—traits that revealed themselves within minutes.

'Organic farming won't give you the yield you're hoping for,' he announced, spitting a neat arc of tobacco juice to the side as if punctuating his point. His tone suggested he'd already decided we were slightly unhinged.

But we held our ground. We'd rather have a smaller, cleaner harvest than compromise on our principles. The earthworms could have their feast, and we'd take whatever came our way.

And so preparations began, with Vishwas leading the way. His first task was a prescribed burn—a controlled fire used to clear dry grass and ready the land for rice nurseries. He worked with the easy rhythm of someone who had done this a hundred times before—setting fire to dry grass in carefully controlled sections, watching the flames curl and dance before stamping them out at the right moment. The smoke rose in thin wisps, carrying with it the scent of charred earth, while the remaining ash was raked into the soil to enrich it before planting.

Our next big decision was what to plant. We chose a mix of traditional and experimental rice varieties. Kolam, a fragrant medium-grain rice commonly grown across Maharashtra, would be our staple. Indrayani, with its slightly sticky texture, was known to cope well with erratic monsoons—perfect for our unpredictable weather. We also included Assamese black rice—the same heirloom variety that had given us an absurdly tiny but morale-boosting harvest the year before. Technically, that victory belonged to the hamlet farmer who had grown it for us, but we clung to it like proud parents anyway. I had tracked down fresh seeds from a collector in the Northeast, and this time the responsibility (and any impending fiasco) was entirely ours. With their deep purple grains and cult-like reputation, the seeds felt less risky now—more like unfinished business.

That black rice, however, came with an embarrassing backstory. Months earlier, I had called the Seedman to finalise the purchase.

'Bhen eez your cantibaishan?' he asked.

'Anytime you say,' I replied confidently, unsure of what he meant.

'How I can say bhen eez your cantibaishan?' he repeated, sounding annoyed.

'Uh ... send me your bank details?' I offered, now panicking.

'Bhay you bhaunt my bhank details?!' he shrieked.

It was only after several mortifying minutes that I realised he was asking about 'cultivation', not 'contribution'.

While I was busy miscommunicating with seed collectors, Sunil had been developing grand visions of mechanised farming. He was determined to hire a high-powered tractor to churn through the fields, leaving behind neat, geometric rows. Unfortunately, our land had other plans. It was wildly uneven, scattered with saplings, boulders and the occasional tree that refused to be relocated. A tractor here would be less 'efficient machinery' and more a 'wrecking ball on wheels'. Reluctantly, we traded horsepower for bull power, opting for a traditional bull-drawn plough—slower, quieter and significantly less destructive.

Now, all we needed was rain.

After days of waiting, the first real downpour arrived. It began gently, soaking the earth and filling the air with rich petrichor. Soon, as if making up for lost time, the skies opened up, turning the bunded fields into shallow, muddy pools. Our feet sank into the softened ground with satisfying squelches as we waded in to inspect the newly formed rice nursery.

Weeks later, the seedlings were ready for transplanting. At 5 a.m., Suzann, Sunil and I loaded up the car, stopping first at Sangam Sweets in Kolad. Farming, we'd learnt, is infinitely more tolerable with a box of fresh sweets in tow.

By the time we reached the farm, Vishwas and his nine-person crew—five women and four men—were already hard at work. Two ploughs, four bulls and a lot of determination had turned our land into a hive of activity. Including our local farmhands and the three of us, there were now sixteen people bustling about.

Harvesting the rice seedlings was another lesson in back-breaking humility. It involved crouching in knee-deep mud, pulling out delicate tufts of green by hand, and tying them into small bundles. Within minutes, we realised why rice farmers have the endurance of Olympians. Our city-style gumboots, which we had proudly donned that morning, were met with amused laughter.

'Those will sink in the mud,' the crew laughed.

They were right. Within minutes, the boots were abandoned, and we waded in barefoot, slipping and stumbling like newborn calves.

As the transplanting began, the women working alongside us broke into song. It was a slow, rhythmic melody, simple yet carrying the weight of generations. The lyrics, in a dialect we didn't fully understand, spoke of the rains, of patience, of harvests yet to come. The men joined in next, their deeper voices adding harmony as they bent, pulled and planted in synchronised rhythm with the land. At first, we only listened, but soon, Suzann and I found ourselves humming along, our awkward attempts at planting falling into step with the song.

At one point, Sunil even attempted to use the cattle plough. Let's just say the bulls were less than impressed, and Vishwas quickly put an end to Sunil's cowboy ambitions.

We were sore, mud-caked and exhausted when we stopped for lunch. The meal, prepared by Mrs Pingle, was waiting in the storage shed—a steaming heap of rice bhakris, chicken curry and a fiery rassa (thin curry), served with onions, lime and green chillies. The curry pots had been buried in a vat of hot rice to keep everything warm, a practical touch that left us city folk duly impressed. We ate in companionable silence, the morning's efforts sitting heavy on our limbs.

After lunch, we passed around sweets, their sugary warmth a small but welcome reward. There was still more work to be done, but for the first time, I felt like we were finding our rhythm. Farming had never been just about planting and harvesting—it was about patience, about moving with nature's cycles rather than against them.

As we packed up for the day and headed back towards Mumbai, the sky darkened again and the road ahead glistened ominously. Sure, the fields were ready for planting, but the highways clearly weren't ready for anything at all.

14

The Road Less Travelled (Because It's Covered in Craters)

August–September 2022

THE MONSOON BROUGHT LIFE TO OUR FARM—AND absolute devastation to the road leading to it.

It was impossible not to notice what the season was doing to the land.

There's something undeniably magical about the monsoon in the Konkan region. The entire landscape transforms into a vivid, almost obnoxiously vibrant shade of green, as if nature has decided to outshine every painter, photographer and filmmaker who has ever dared to capture its beauty. The hills glow, the trees glisten and even the scraggliest shrubs look as though they've been groomed by an overenthusiastic celestial gardener.

And then there's the air—oh, the air! It carries the unmistakable fragrance of crushed leaves, damp soil and tender new shoots, a scent so intoxicating it could probably be bottled and sold as 'Konkan No. 5'. Mist rolls in during the early mornings like an overzealous stagehand, draping everything in soft, pearly curtains, and the fields come alive with farmers sowing paddy. Soon, the land becomes a living tapestry, emerald waves stretching all the way to the Sahyadris.

It is so picturesque you'd think you were inside a watercolour painting.

But here's the thing about watercolour paintings—they don't come with highways. And it's the highways that shatter the dream.

Our farm lies 135 kilometres away from Mumbai—a distance that sounds reasonable until you factor in the state of the roads. The first 50 kilometres lull you into a false sense of security. You glide over the Vashi toll bridge, breeze through Navi Mumbai traffic, and merge onto NH48, a smooth stretch of road on which your car purrs with efficiency. It's the kind of highway that makes you believe you've got this whole farming commute figured out.

And then you meet NH66. NH66 is where optimism goes to die.

It's not a highway—it's an elaborate endurance test designed to challenge vehicles, drivers and one's mental health alike. Officially, NH66 ranks as the ninth-longest highway in India, a sprawling artery of asphalt that runs from Panvel in Maharashtra all the way down to Kanyakumari, the country's southernmost tip, winding along the western coastline. The stretch we travel—from Panvel to Kolad—feels like the highway's neglected problem child, left to fend for itself while its better-behaved siblings enjoy the perks of progress and development. Every week, we navigate its battered terrain with a mix of resignation and determination.

The four-laning of NH66 was announced with great fanfare in 2011, promising smoother drives and faster commutes. Yet, over a decade later, the project remains a work in progress—or more accurately, a lack of progress. While other sections have experienced patches of improvement, our stretch of the highway appears to have been entirely forgotten. What remains is a chaotic mishmash of potholes, collapsing shoulders and the occasional construction equipment rusting quietly under the elements.

During the monsoon, this stretch transforms into an outright disaster zone. The relentless rains wash away freshly laid asphalt, leaving potholes multiplying at an alarming rate, turning into craters deep enough to entertain thoughts of scuba diving. The road's edges crumble away, daring anyone to test the limits of their vehicle's suspension. On one particularly ill-conceived patch, someone thought paver blocks would be a viable solution—for a national highway. Unsurprisingly, they didn't hold up. Now, they lie shattered and loose, adding yet another layer of chaos to an already miserable commute.

One particularly memorable morning, we encountered a scene that could only be described as comically tragic. A massive pit had opened up across the entire width of the road, filled with rainwater that shimmered ominously in the dim light. Cars were stopped in their tracks, drivers huddled around the edge of the pit, debating who would be the first fool to attempt a crossing.

'How deep do you think it is?' Sunil mused, peering at the murky water.

'Deep enough to have its own ecosystem,' I replied.

'Or its own PIN code,' Suzann muttered.

Nobody wanted to test the depth, until one brave—or foolish—soul decided to try. His car made it halfway through before sinking into a slurry of muck, requiring much pushing, pulling and cursing to free it. Eventually, another driver led the way, inching across like Indiana Jones navigating a rope bridge, while the rest of us followed in single file, hoping desperately to make it across safely. It was the kind of bonding experience that makes you seriously question your life choices.

Multiply this ordeal by a hundred, and you'll understand why what should be a breezy two-and-a-half-hour drive now takes closer to three-and-a-half hours—on a good day. By the time we reach the farm, we're frazzled, stiff-necked and carrying the physical and emotional scars of the journey. Sunil and I weren't always this jaded, though. Back when we first started our farm adventure, NH66 was passable, even pleasant. We envisioned easy weekend drives, the kind where you roll down the windows, let the wind play with your hair and hum along to a carefully curated playlist. That dream has long since been replaced by the harsh reality of pothole navigation and suspension repair bills.

I've tried everything to draw attention to this crumbling stretch of road. Complaints have been filed, tweets sent and a viral #FixNH66 campaign launched in a desperate attempt. However, the highway appears to exist in a bureaucratic black hole, where maintenance requests often go unaddressed. A few brave souls have taken up the cause, including a lawyer from Raigad who commutes daily to Vashi. He filed a public interest litigation in the Bombay High Court, demanding repairs and the completion of the four-laning project. The court agreed, issuing directives to the National Highways Authority of India (NHAI). But, much like the road itself, those directives appear to have crumbled under the weight of neglect.

'Maybe we should hire someone to stage a protest,' Suzann suggested one afternoon as we bounced over yet another massive pothole.

'Or we could just plant trees in the potholes,' Sunil offered.

'Great idea,' I said. 'At least then they'd get some attention.'

In the meantime, we continue to endure this treacherous stretch, constantly reevaluating how often we can visit the farm without losing our car's undercarriage. One week, after an especially harrowing drive, we experimented with an alternate route. It was thirty kilometres longer but mercifully less brutal, which, by NH66 standards, felt like a win.

As infuriating as the journey is, there's a stubborn part of me that refuses to let it overshadow the magic of the farm. Yes, the road is awful. Yes, it's a logistical nightmare. But every time we finally make it to the farm, surrounded by the lush Konkan greenery and the distant Sahyadris, it feels worth it. There's something grounding about the land, something that makes the chaos fade into the background.

Still, if anyone out there has the ear of the road repair gods—or perhaps knows a particularly motivated minister—please, send them our way. Until then, the farm will remain our little oasis, a patch of peace and promise that we'll keep fighting for, one pothole at a time.

But as we kept navigating that battered highway week after week, none of us realised the farm was cooking up its own surprise—one that would make even NH66 look forgiving.

15

Kharif Harvest: The Rice Reality Check

November 2022

By November 2022, we finally understood what the land had been plotting all along.

The roads were still a menace—but the paddy fields didn't care. They stood tall, golden, and utterly ready for harvest.

The farm had transformed entirely. The fields we had painstakingly prepared in June now bowed under the weight of ripening grain. The bunds had dried and cracked in the post-monsoon sun, the air smelled faintly of hay, and our harvest crew was already gathering at the edge of the field—sickles sharpened, gamchas tied, ready for the first cut.

This was our first real kharif harvest, the first time the land would show us what months of mud, sweat and slightly confused decision-making had amounted to. And because optimism remained our most abundant crop, we arrived armed with enthusiastic yield estimates and visions of heaving rice sacks that we were convinced would soon line the shed. Sunil had picked up an intriguing statistic from his school friend Dinesh, who exported farm equipment to Nigeria and Ghana. According to Dinesh, with fertile soil, chemical inputs and mechanised tools, rice yields could go as high as 3,000 kilograms per acre. We cross-checked the figure on Google and, even at a conservative estimate—say, half that—we calculated that our one-and-a-half-acre plot could still produce around 2,250 kilograms of paddy. After dehusking, that would leave us with roughly 1,125 kilograms of rice. Over a metric tonne. Despite our obvious lack of experience, we remained undeterred. Optimism is a stubborn creature, and ours had latched onto a very specific vision: overflowing rice sacks, logistical nightmares of abundance and the distinct possibility of needing a truck to transport our bounty.

We were farmers! Or at least, we were playing the part. The rice had grown tall, swaying gracefully in the monsoon breeze, glowing with the promise of a successful harvest. Each visit to the farm felt like a victory lap. We admired the lush green expanse, snapped dramatic photos and even debated packaging options. Sunil floated the idea of a custom farm logo. Suzann suggested rustic, hand-stitched labels. I envisioned the tagline: 'Grown with love and mild incompetence'.

Then reality tapped us on the shoulder with a raised eyebrow, like it had been watching us the whole time while munching on popcorn, particularly amused by the fact that our entire farming knowledge came from Google. One afternoon, as we stood in the midst of our flourishing fields, Sunil turned to Vishwas.

'How much yield can we expect? Should I organise a truck?' he asked, his voice a blend of cautious optimism and barely contained excitement.

Vishwas, ever the realist, squinted at the field. 'Seven quintals, perhaps.'

Seven quintals. Seven. That amounted to 700 kilograms of paddy—less than half the national average per acre. I stared at him, waiting for the punchline. Surely he meant seven tonnes?

Sunil, ever the optimist, nodded enthusiastically. 'That's still quite substantial.'

Grim Sanjay, forever the harbinger of doom, let out a low, incredulous chuckle. 'Seven quintals?' he snorted. 'From this rocky soil? And with organic methods?' He shook his head. 'Don't dream so big. Even one quintal would be a miracle.'

Suzann and I exchanged glances, unwilling to let his doom-and-gloom attitude ruin the moment. Seven quintals still sounded like a lot—enough to fill our pantry, gift generously and maybe even earn some bragging rights. We ignored Sanjay's warnings. The rice looked fantastic. Surely the soil couldn't be that bad?

As the weeks progressed, the Kolam rice was the first to blush golden, followed closely by the Indrayani. The millets ripened next—eager, quick and wonderfully uncomplicated. The Assamese black rice lingered loftily at the back, fully aware of its heirloom status and in no particular hurry to join the common crowd.

Even as the fields were ready for harvest, Vishwas—predictably—was not. He had evaporated, leaving behind increasingly creative excuses.

'My aunt is sick,' he said one morning.

'The cattle need tending,' he claimed the next.

Eventually, he stopped answering his phone altogether.

Left to our own devices, we roped in Maruti, his wife and a few of his friends to help manage the harvest. Together, we cut, bundled and stacked the Kolam, black rice, nachni and sama—working our way through the fields one slow, sweaty patch at a time. It wasn't elegant, but it got the job done.

By this point, we'd adjusted our expectations. No trucks. No iconic harvest photos. No cinematic scenes of grain cascading from sacks. But surely there'd still be enough to fill the boot of our car?

Right?

And now, for the grand total:

- 30 kilograms of Kolam rice
- 10 kilograms of Indrayani rice
- 7 kilograms of black rice (from 10 kilograms of seeds)
- 35 kilograms of nachni
- 13 kilograms of sama

That was 47 kilograms of rice. From an entire acre. Less than a hundredth of what we had naively envisioned.

Sunil bent down and picked up a handful of rice. 'So,' he said slowly, turning to me, 'should I book the truck now?'

I glared at him. It was the farming equivalent of being hit in the face with a wet sock.

Naturally, Grim Sanjay wasted no time. His 'I told you so' was delivered with the kind of smug satisfaction usually reserved for cricket commentators who've correctly predicted a batting collapse five overs in advance. The farm crew muttered among themselves, shaking their heads at our organic ambitions.

Mahesh, who had heroically restrained himself until now, finally spoke. 'Maybe a little urea and chemical fertiliser wouldn't hurt next time,' he said, gently.

I turned to him. 'You don't say.'

Still clinging to denial, I called a friend, a homestay owner and enthusiastic farmer in Kanha to share my woes. He listened patiently and then asked one devastatingly simple question: 'Did you test the soil?'

Soil testing! Of course. The one thing we hadn't considered.

Our friend advised us to analyse the soil's nutrient levels to see what was missing and whether we could replenish them organically. And so, we became soil detectives, collecting samples like forensic experts and delivering them to the R&D division of Rashtriya Chemicals and Fertilisers Ltd. (a government manufacturing company). The results would tell us whether our rice-growing dreams were salvageable—or if we should finally listen to Grim Sanjay and plant mangoes instead.

While we waited for the soil results, one day Sunil turned to me with a straight face. 'Maybe we should still rent a truck,' he said. 'Purely for the drama.'

I stared at him. 'Sunil ... our entire harvest can fit in the back seat of the car. With room for snacks.'

He shrugged. 'Fine. A pickup? A tempo? Something?'

'At this rate,' I said, 'even two reusable grocery bags feel generous.'

We laughed—partly at the absurdity of it all, partly at ourselves. Farming had made one thing abundantly clear: disaster was inevitable, humility was compulsory, and the only reliable yield was the stories we'd collect along the way.

16

Turmeric, the Plant that Refused to Die

December 2022

THE MOMENT THE KHARIF HARVEST WAS BEHIND US, WE plunged straight into winter planting. There was no time to brood; the farm refused to pause just because our pride had taken a beating. Wheat, bajra, sweet corn and a parade of vegetables—brinjals, tomatoes, chillies, even watermelon—were sown with the grim determination of people who had learnt not to make eye contact with hope.

Success with methi, mooli and coriander brought a flicker of satisfaction, but we didn't allow ourselves to get carried away. This was a farm, not a balcony garden. 'Mildly pleased' was the highest emotion permitted.

Somewhere on the periphery of all this activity lay a patch we had collectively abandoned: turmeric. Planted in the monsoon, its once lush green leaves had shrivelled into sad brown flags by mid-October. By November, the whole section resembled an archaeological site—silent, cracked and, as far as I was concerned, dead. After the kharif fiasco, mourning another crop felt unnecessary. So we didn't. We simply looked the other way and focused on what still had a fighting chance.

Weeks passed. The winter sun grew sharper. Every other crop demanded attention. The turmeric remained untouched, undisturbed and wholly uninteresting.

Then one day, while debating where to plant the bajra, Maruti casually mentioned something that made me stop in my tracks. 'We need to harvest the turmeric first,' he said offhandedly.

'Harvest the turmeric?' I blinked. Surely I'd misheard. The turmeric had died, hadn't it?

Curiosity got the better of me, so we trudged over to the overlooked patch. What happened next belongs in a small, triumphant corner of our farm's mythology.

To my surprise—and slight embarrassment—there they were: rows of plump turmeric roots hiding under brittle, lifeless leaves. As it turns out, turmeric is *meant* to look dead before it's ready for harvest; the leaves turn yellow, then brown, then collapse entirely, concealing an underground world that continues quietly doing its job.

Before I could process this revelation, Maruti plunged his hand into the soil, gave a dramatic tug—and out came a thick, golden knuckle of turmeric, dusted with earth and absolutely magnificent. Then another. And another.

Hidden beneath the desolate surface was a treasure trove of halad—bright, fragrant and stubbornly alive. A crop we had written off as a failure had been thriving underground, following its own timeline, entirely indifferent to our neglect and theatrical assumptions.

'Who knew?' I murmured.

Maruti raised an eyebrow. 'Me.'

Right. Clearly, my disillusionment with rice had blinded me to this humble patch of hope.

Maruti and his wife got to work, their efficiency a marvel. In no time, they'd dug up one-and-a-half kilograms of fresh, fragrant turmeric—a modest haul, but a victory nonetheless. We weren't exactly triumphant rice barons, but hey, becoming turmeric-growers wasn't a bad fallback.

Fresh turmeric is delightful, but transforming it into powder is another matter altogether. Enter Google, along with some guidance from my mum's house help. First, the turmeric had to be cured. After a thorough scrubbing, I boiled the roots, with scum bubbling to the surface, until the kitchen smelled like a bustling spice market.

'This gelatinises the starch,' Google claimed, 'intensifies the colour and ensures uniformity.'

Once boiled, the roots needed slicing—thinly, evenly and painstakingly. This was no small task, but my Fitbit thought it was fabulous. It logged three-and-a-half kilometres of 'steps', fifty-five minutes of activity and 1,000 calories burnt, all while I stood in one spot chopping turmeric. If only all exercise were this easy.

Drying the turmeric was simple enough—just a matter of letting it sunbathe like a retiree on a budget beach holiday. The sliced turmeric was laid out on trays and placed on the balcony to dry. For an entire week, the slices basked in the sun, crisping up until they snapped cleanly in two.

Grinding it into powder, though? That was the tricky part.

Traditionally, there are two methods for grinding spices. The first is the piston method, in which spices are pulverised by repetitive, rhythmic pounding. Back in the day, this job was often handled by women who would show up at your building or colony armed with stout lathis and a wooden bucket. They'd pour the spices in and proceed to hammer away with a vigour that made you suspect they were working out some personal grievances.

The second method involves using a set of grinding wheels, the more refined, mechanised cousin of the wooden bucket. This was the domain of spice mills, but alas, a quick survey revealed that all the local spice mills had shut shop. Even the legendary Bandra Bazaar spice shop admitted, somewhat sheepishly, that they no longer ground their own spices.

With no lathis, buckets or grinding wheels in sight, what was a determined turmeric enthusiast to do?

Enter the Vitamix. Sunil, always the pragmatist, declared, 'If it can crush ice, it can handle turmeric.'

I hesitated, worried about staining the blender jar or dulling the blades, but practicality won out. Five glorious minutes later, we had the finest, most vibrant turmeric powder I'd ever seen. After running it through a sieve and giving it one last whirl in the blender, the result was a silky-smooth, golden powder.

From our humble one-and-a-half kilograms of fresh turmeric, we ended up with 400 grams of turmeric powder. Not a massive yield, but considering we'd written off the crop as a failure, it felt like an absolute triumph.

Buoyed by this unexpected success, we decided to give turmeric its rightful due. Next year, in June 2023, we planted it again—properly this time, in neat rows, with the kind of care usually reserved for firstborn children and fragile egos. By early 2024, the leaves had begun to yellow, and Suzann and I were ready to pounce with sickles in hand.

But Maruti stood his ground. 'Not this year,' he said firmly, crossing his arms with the authority of someone who had personally mentored each rhizome. 'Let it stay. Next year—*fat halad.*'

And so, for once, we listened.

At the time of writing, that turmeric still lies beneath the soil, quietly thickening (we hope), gathering strength for what Maruti assures us will be a 'bumper' harvest. Whether that confidence is based on experience, instinct or sheer optimism is anyone's guess—but for now, we choose to believe him.

After all, turmeric has already surprised us once.

Now we wondered, if turmeric could surprise us, what else might the farm be hiding? As we set our sights on new crops, memories of old ones came rushing back—ones that didn't need sieves or blenders, just a little salt, some boiling water and a child's unbridled joy.

YEAR THREE: 2023

17

Ditch the Edamame

February 2023

YEAR THREE ARRIVED WITH A STRANGE, UNEXPECTED tug—a childhood memory resurfacing without warning.

Some childhood memories drift away like sand through your fingers, but others stick stubbornly, remaining as vivid as if they happened yesterday. For me, one such memory involves two great loves: Nancy Drew mysteries and a large bowl of something far more compelling than any plot twist—cold, salty, utterly delicious boiled toor, or pigeon peas. Not some exotic bean or fancy superfood—just plain old toor, boil in salted water and served cold.

At the time, I had no idea what I was eating, nor did I care. All I knew was that it was the best snack ever. Whenever my mum boiled a large batch, I'd look forward to it with the same giddy excitement I felt before a holiday. The moment that pot hit the kitchen counter, I was there, abandoning my book mid-sentence to grab a handful of damp, wrinkled pods.

The pods were dark brown, wet, salty and gloriously messy. I'd strip the beans with my teeth, relishing the pop as they broke free, savouring the salt as it clung to my tongue. One pod led to another, and soon my book would be forgotten, my hands getting sticky from the salty residue, and an impressive pile of discarded pods lying in front of me like some strange shrine to gluttony. There was something immensely satisfying about the whole ritual—the peeling, the crunch, the rush of salt on my lips. The pleasure was as much in the process as in the taste.

And yet, despite my deep, almost religious devotion to boiled toor, my young brain never connected it to the toor dal that graced our plates every week. How could something so divine transform into that bland yellow mush? To me, they were entirely different species. One was heaven, and the other ... a compulsory sidekick to my roti, barely tolerated.

But as childhood snacks often do, boiled toor faded away, replaced by more convenient, ready-made alternatives. The kind of snacks that didn't involve saltwater dripping down your chin or a heap of messy pods gathering like evidence of a crime scene. The humble toor quietly vanished from my snacking habits, lying dormant in memory, until the day the world inexplicably crowned edamame as the trendiest thing ever to grace a menu.

You know where this is going, don't you?

One fine evening, many years ago, I found myself at a swanky Japanese restaurant, its dim lighting and soft jazz working overtime to justify the eye-watering prices. A waiter ceremoniously plonked a bowl of steamed edamame on the table, its bright green pods gleaming under the warm glow of a low-hanging lamp. As I stared at them, a faint tingle of recognition stirred at the back of my mind.

One bite, and it hit me. The taste, the texture, the pod-popping joy—it was exactly like eating boiled toor. My childhood snack, just greener and pricier.

'Edamame is just trendy toor!' I blurted out, possibly louder than restaurant etiquette allowed.

Sunil looked up from his menu, unimpressed. 'Are you sure? It doesn't seem the same.'

'It is! Look at it—it's just green! They've dressed up our toor, given it a Japanese name, and now it's a luxury item!'

He popped a pod into his mouth and chewed. 'Hmm. I don't know. It's softer. Less ... earthy.'

'That's because it's a soybean. But the experience is the same! They stole our toor's moment!'

Sunil sighed. 'You're taking this very personally.'

'I *am* taking this personally! I spent my childhood happily chomping on toor, and now this—' I jabbed at the edamame pod, 'this is what's considered cool?'

We agreed to disagree, and I continued ordering edamame for years, all while nursing the secret knowledge that toor had done it first.

Fast forward to March 2021: Two Bandra Girls Bought a Farm.

One day, as Mahesh rattled off a list of crops to be planted, he casually mentioned toor. I nodded absentmindedly, still distracted by the ongoing soap opera that was our rice crop. Several months later, during a walk through the fields, Mahesh pointed to some blooming bushes. Delicate pink flowers adorned the plants, and hanging from them were green pods—slightly fuzzy and heartbreakingly familiar.

'You can boil these when they're tender,' Mahesh said.

And that's when it all clicked.

This was my toor. The messy, salty pods of my childhood, growing right here on our farm. The realisation was like stumbling upon a treasure chest of memories, except instead of jewels, it was filled with delicious legumes.

Over the next few visits, we harvested basketfuls, and I rekindled my love affair with those salty little beans. Each bite transported me back to a simpler time, when life revolved around books and snacks, and no one was trying to charge ₹600 for a bowl of pods.

Which begs the question: why has toor stayed a secret?

India produces nearly 90 per cent of the world's pigeon peas. That's right—toor is our thing. Yet somehow, this brilliant snack has never made it past home kitchens, quietly eclipsed by edamame, the green pretender. Restaurant menus everywhere feature imported edamame, charging anywhere from ₹500 to ₹800 for a pitiful bowl of pods.

It's ludicrous. A kilo of fresh toor pods costs ₹125. That's enough to feed your entire family, neighbours and maybe even a few stray cats. Edamame, on the other hand, comes frozen, is shipped across oceans and steamed into a pricey bowl of hipster hype.

And let's talk nutrition. Toor is packed with protein, fibre and more vitamins than I can count—a true overachiever. Edamame? It just sits there looking smug, charging a premium for its trendy green coat.

Here's the kicker: toor has been a star of folk medicine for centuries. It's said to cure everything from gingivitis to oral ulcers, and even helps with lactation (although I haven't personally tested this claim). Yet, it's ignored, while edamame lounges on fancy tables, basking in the glow of undeserved adoration.

Now for the pitch: it's time to reclaim our toor. Restaurateurs, are you listening? Ditch the imported pods and give us back our salty, messy, joy-inducing snack. Let's make boiled toor the next big thing—it's local, delicious and costs less than your morning chai.

As for me, I'm happy to polish off a bowl of cold, salty toor, curled up with a book, just like the good old days. Nancy Drew might not join me, but these pods? They're back for good, and this time, I know exactly what I'm eating.

I suppose that's the thing about life—it has a way of circling back when you least expect it. The farm has given me plenty of lessons in patience, resilience and in the fine art of laughing at my own mistakes, but more than anything, it has reminded me that some joys never truly disappear. They just wait for the right moment to return.

And if boiled toor can find its way back to me after all these years, who's to say what else might be waiting just around the corner?

In our case, what waited was the farm—demanding as ever, tugging us back into its colourful, chaotic orbit.

18

Colour Me Red

March 2023

Farm visits for us aren't tranquil escapes; they're chaotic military operations with a touch of comedy. The first battle? Juggling schedules—a feat that feels like auditioning for a circus act. Suzann's work deadlines, Sunil's 'emergency' meetings and my to-do list, which grows faster than weeds, all need to align in some rare celestial event. When the stars finally cooperate, we gear up for a day that promises anything but rest.

Whether it's wrangling with the electricity guys, deciphering the whims of a government surveyor or accompanying the village water diviner as he 'converses' with underground streams, the agenda is always a mix of the absurd and the unavoidable.

But every so often, something extraordinary happens: a farm visit with no specific agenda. No to-do lists, no bureaucratic puzzles, just a day to breathe.

Tuesday, 7 March 2023, was one of those rare gems. It was Holi, the festival of colour, and for once, the roads were eerily empty. No blaring horns, no monstrous trucks overtaking like they were auditioning for *Mad Max*, and no motorcyclists zipping past as though the highway were their personal video game. The drive was unusually smooth, almost unnervingly so, as if the universe had decided to lull us into a rare moment of calm before springing its next surprise.

Joining us was Archana, a fellow farm enthusiast and the self-appointed purveyor of snacks, armed with enough Tupperware to stage a mid-journey buffet. We cruised along in relative bliss, revelling in the rare quiet of Holi traffic—or lack thereof—until we turned onto the dirt road leading to the farm and encountered our first obstacle: a Holi roadblock.

A group of young boys, faces smeared in a kaleidoscope of colours, stood defiantly in the middle of the road, clutching a bamboo stick like sentries guarding entry to a medieval castle. Their expressions were equal parts glee and determination, as though they'd been cast in a low-budget film as the protectors of sacred treasure.

We stopped the car, exchanged glances and waited. The boys stared back at us with the same intensity.

'What's happening?' Sunil muttered, squinting at them like they were rare birds spotted on a wildlife safari.

I cautiously rolled down the window. 'Kay ...?'

The boys just continued to stare at us, clearly baffled by our inability to grasp what was happening.

Eventually, an older onlooker strolled up, trying his hardest not to laugh.

'They want Holi cha pos,' he said, enjoying our confusion a bit too much.

Ah, Holi tax—a quirky rural tradition where, during Holi, children block the road and demand a small toll to let you pass, playfully hinting that refusal might result in you being doused in vibrant colours.

Laughing, we handed over a small bribe and, with great ceremony, the bamboo stick was lifted. We waved as we drove on, mildly charmed by the spectacle.

The charm wore off quickly.

Two hundred meters later, another posse appeared, this time with an even sturdier bamboo barricade and expressions that clearly said, 'You're not getting through without paying up.'

Suzann sighed, 'We should've stocked up on coins,' as we reluctantly handed over more Holi tax to the pint-sized highwaymen. Their grins stretched wide as they pocketed the cash, a combination of triumph and mischief dancing in their eyes.

By the time we reached the farm, we had navigated nine roadblocks in just eight kilometres. With every stop, the demands grew more theatrical, and we were practically flinging change out of the window by the end, much to the delight of these tiny extortionists.

Sunil, gripping the steering wheel like it was the last thread of his patience, muttered darkly, 'If I see another bamboo stick ...'

But the farm, as always, had its way of soothing tempers.

Maruti, with his characteristic wide grin and his perpetually cheerful wife, greeted us at the gate, their arms laden with baskets overflowing with freshly plucked tomatoes and aubergines. The vegetables, still warm from the sun, glowed like treasures, their vibrant colours a feast for the eyes.

The farm hummed with quiet contentment—rustling leaves and distant bird calls blending into a symphony of calm.

Unlike the kharif season, when the land is at the mercy of an unpredictable monsoon, rabi season is a quieter, more calculated affair. It begins in October–November, after the rains have receded, leaving behind soil that is drier but still holding on to some of the season's moisture. These are the months when wheat, tomatoes, watermelon and chilli take centre stage—crops that don't demand downpours but instead thrive on carefully rationed irrigation. If kharif is a dramatic gamble played against the forces of nature, rabi is the thinking farmer's season—a time when decisions about water management, crop choice and field preparation carry just as much weight as the planting itself. The fields are no longer drowned in rain but sculpted with precision, tilled into orderly furrows that yield grain, vegetables and fruit.

For us, rabi meant a fresh start—a chance to recover from our monsoon mishaps, reassess what the land was willing to offer and plant crops that relied less on luck and more on careful planning.

Harvesting tomatoes proved unexpectedly therapeutic. Their ruby-red skins glistened under the sun, and plucking them straight from the vine felt like gathering small treasures.

Then came the watermelons—a delightful harvesting session that turned into a contest of who could master the art of knocking to test them for ripeness. Did you know watermelons on the vine are naturally cool to the touch? Really, palpably cool. In the blazing sun, they felt like tiny miracles. I, of course, had to google this later because who am I if not someone who needs to know the 'why' behind everything? It turns out that watermelons have high water content, which gives them high specific heat capacity and helps keep them cool. Farming is full of unexpected science lessons.

By the end of the day, our haul was impressive: baskets of tomatoes, watermelons, aubergines, chillies, cashews and a handful of peculiar Malabar cucumbers that looked like alien artefacts. Also known as 'chow chow' across South India, these curious vegetables added to the eclectic mix of our harvest.

There's a quiet satisfaction in seeing the literal fruits of your labour—a reminder that this chaotic, unpredictable venture was worth every challenge.

The drive back, predictably, featured familiar faces at the Holi roadblocks, ready for round two.

But this time, we were seasoned pros. 'Already paid!' Sunil shouted as he accelerated past their confused grins. It felt like a small but meaningful triumph.

As the sun sank low, bathing the fields in soft light, we savoured the memory of a day without urgent tasks or bureaucratic hurdles—just simple, unhurried joy.

Farming humbled us. It reminded us that no matter how much we planned, debated or resisted, the land had the final say. Yet, in those fleeting moments—when the fields stood golden, the harvest lay heavy in our hands and the sky stretched wide above us—it felt as though we were slowly learning its language. There would be more seasons, more roadblocks and more experiments that straddled the line between brilliant and absurd. We drove home that evening, our hands stained with tomato juice and the car laden with the day's harvest; a quiet, rare kind of joy after a day spent exactly how it was meant to be.

Today, the land had offered its best. What came next—well, that would be the beginning of our Google-Lens phase, though we didn't know it yet.

All we knew was we'd be back, again and again, but especially every Holi.

For the laughter.

For the pos.

And for the harvest in every shade of red.

19

Google Lens Farming

March 2023

HERE'S A QUESTION I NEVER THOUGHT I'D ASK: HOW DID anyone farm before Google Lens?

Go ahead, laugh—I'm laughing too, but mostly at myself. Sure, there's the whole romantic notion of wisdom of the ages, where farming knowledge gets passed down like a prized heirloom. Lovely idea, really. But what do you do when your lineage includes zero farmers, and your strongest ancestral skill is finding Bandra's best brunch spot?

Enter Google Lens: the app that took our amateur-hour farming misadventures and upgraded them to ... well, slightly less embarrassing misadventures.

And if you're wondering what it actually does, Google Lens works like a pair of supercharged detective eyes built into your phone. You simply point your camera—or take a quick photo—and it searches the internet for lookalikes. It compares your image to millions of others and tells you what it might be, where it's from, what it's used for and sometimes even where to buy it.

In short, it's the app that rescues clueless adults from themselves.

And for two city slickers attempting to farm, Google Lens didn't just help. It became the only one on the team who actually knew what it was doing.

Take the time Mahesh casually dismissed a field of delicate blooms as 'monsoon rubbish'. Suzann and I exchanged horrified glances—those flowers deserved better than his disdain. Determined to uncover their true worth, we turned to our trusted ally. One photo later, Google Lens revealed the truth: these weren't weeds but wild turmeric flowers, heralding a treasure trove of medicinal turmeric rhizomes buried beneath. We unearthed them with triumphant grins, feeling vindicated and just a tad smug.

Then there was the giant blue scorpion incident.

Picture this: a majestic, ominous-looking creature crawling across the farm, commanding respect and fear in equal measure. Most people would've run for the hills. Not us. We leaned in, snapped a photo and let Google Lens do its magic. Within seconds, we had a name: *Heterometrus spinifer*, or, as it's more commonly known, the giant blue scorpion.

'Is it venomous?' I asked.

Suzann, scrolling through the results, shrugged. 'Mildly.'

'Mildly? What does that even mean?'

'Means you probably won't die.'

Oh, well, in that case.

Google Lens turned out to be our wildlife Sherlock Holmes, arriving just in time to identify creatures, unravel their backstories and occasionally warn us about their lethal tendencies. We used it to confirm the presence of the peninsular rock agama—a lizard that looked like it had escaped from Jurassic Park—and to identify a suspiciously enthusiastic snake that had taken up residence near our tool shed. Harmless, Google assured us. Unless provoked—which, unfortunately, was our default mode.

And when even Google Lens has no answers, we rely on our friend Surya, our unofficial wildlife hotline, who gracefully endures my steady stream of WhatsApp photos, each helpfully captioned, 'Who dis?'

But Google Lens wasn't just about wildlife—it saved us time and time again on the farm. Like the time we forgot what we'd planted in the far corner of the field. Something medicinal ... maybe? One quick scan, and voilà: black turmeric, otherwise known as *Curcuma caesia*. Another win for tech-assisted farming.

Even the most unexpected crops benefited from our digital detective work. Take Malabar cucumbers—initially dismissed as weird-looking veggies, they turned out to be a powerhouse of nutrients with unexpected culinary versatility. Suddenly, what seemed like a pile of farm oddities became part of recipes waiting to be conjured. Suzann, embracing the absurdity, started calling us the Lens Farmers, claiming that without the app, we'd probably be farming glorified weeds.

But the app's finest hour came during the tomato season of March 2023.

Weeks of daily updates from Maruti—photos, progress reports and the occasional unsolicited opinion—made it clear that the tomatoes were thriving, plump, green and brimming with promise. Then, out of nowhere, radio silence.

Three days without a single peep from Maruti felt like an eternity, changing our optimism into slow-boiling dread.

'Why hasn't he sent any pictures?' Suzann asked, eyeing her phone suspiciously.

I shrugged. 'Maybe he's busy?'

Sunil shook his head. 'Or maybe something's wrong.'

Finally, we tracked him down, only for him to send a single photo accompanied by an ominous mutter: 'Problems.'

When someone like Maruti, master of exaggerated complaints, gets that cryptic, you know you're in trouble.

The sight was gut-wrenching: small, black, leathery spots had formed at the base of several tomatoes, their once-smooth green surfaces now marred and uninviting. It was like discovering a scratch on a brand-new car—only worse, because these tomatoes were months of sweat, hope and optimism in the making.

Panic kicked in. Was this some devastating blight that would wipe out our entire crop? Could this be the end of our brief flirtation with agricultural glory?

Before we could spiral into despair, I did what any self-respecting novice farmer would do—I turned to Google Lens.

Within seconds, it spat out a diagnosis: blossom end rot (BER).

It sounded like the botanical equivalent of a death sentence, but a quick dive into the search results told a different story. BER wasn't as catastrophic as it looked. The culprit? Inconsistent watering and a calcium deficiency. In other words, our tomatoes were stressed out and undernourished—problems we could fix.

Armed with this newfound wisdom, we wasted no time. We regulated the watering schedule with military precision and applied a calcium boost to the soil. Crisis averted, the tomatoes got their spa treatment, and we clung to the hope of a comeback.

Our quick response paid off. Weeks later, our tomatoes were thriving again, and we harvested over seventy kilos of ripe, juicy tomatoes.

But that success brought a new problem: what do you do with seventy kilos of tomatoes? Handing them out to neighbours like oversized Halloween candy wasn't practical. Letting them rot wasn't an option.

And so Suzann channelled her inner culinary diva. 'These tomatoes,' she announced, surveying our bounty with the air of a seasoned chef, 'are far too special for subji.'

Sunil and I exchanged a wary glance. 'Okay ...'

'We're making marinara sauce.'

What followed was not a graceful, sunlit, Instagram-worthy cooking session. It was a full-scale operation.

First came the washing. The tomatoes, still covered in farm dust, were rinsed repeatedly until they gleamed. Then came the chopping—an endless, monotonous cycle that quickly made us question whether we had severely underestimated just how much seventy kilos of tomatoes really were.

Before we could even begin cooking, we had another task: finding the right jars. Enter the wholesale glass bottle shop in Crawford Market, our saviour in bulk packaging.

As the tomatoes cooked down in massive pots, the kitchen turned into a fragrant steam bath. Sunil, wielding his wooden spoon like a maestro, tasted, adjusted and refined the sauce as though he were crafting a masterpiece. Garlic sizzled in olive oil, fresh basil leaves were ceremoniously tossed in, and the scent of simmering tomatoes filled the house.

'This,' Sunil declared, peering into a bubbling pot, 'is going to be epic.'

And he wasn't wrong. The sauce thickened into a rich, deep-red masterpiece. Ladles of it were transferred into sterilised jars, their contents a glossy swirl of tangy tomato, aromatic garlic and the faintest hint of farm-grown basil. When the lids were sealed and the labels stuck on, they stood proudly on the counter—batches of marinara officially christened under the 'Two Bandra Girls' brand. Friends and family were promptly recruited as taste-testers—a strategy that doubled as a thinly veiled attempt to offload jars. The verdict? Glowing. Some even dubbed us 'culinary geniuses', a title Sunil accepted with a modest yet suspiciously smug smile. Suzann and I didn't mind riding his coat-tails; after all, our job had been equal parts cheerleading and crisis management.

The crowning moment came when the Two Bandra Girls were unofficially declared winners of the 'World ka Best Marinara Sauce' contest. Sunil's recipe, of course, was the star of the show, and we basked shamelessly in the glory. Each jar became a badge of honour.

'Oh, this? Just a little something we whipped up with our farm-fresh tomatoes,' we'd say, conveniently omitting the frantic Googling, bouts of doubt and general tomato-related mayhem that had paved the way.

That night, as we sat down to plates of pasta drenched in our homemade sauce, we marvelled at how far we'd come.

Farming wasn't just about solving problems, it was about savouring the messy, unpredictable journey that came with them.

And, as always, the farm wasn't done with us.

Because what came next was hotter, heavier, and infinitely more complicated.

The kind of heat that didn't just scorch the fields—it got under the skin.

20

The Heat is On

April 2023

April arrived with its usual swagger, dragging a heatwave with it. The sun came up swinging, blazing from the moment it rose, and by mid-morning the air already rippled with the kind of heat that clings to your skin and turns even small tasks into endurance tests.

Before the heat spiked tempers and logic alike, it was worth admitting something: by Year Three, we finally had something resembling a rhythm.

Kharif sowing (June to October) had us knee-deep in rice and millet, even as climbers like gourds and pumpkins wrapped themselves around trellises in satisfying symmetry.

Rabi (November to May) brought the promise of wheat, corn, tomatoes and enough greens to rival a Bandra salad bar. Routine had become a welcome friend—predictable, comforting and essential.

But at the farm, the real heat wasn't in the weather; it simmered in the tempers, the frustrations and in the constant tug-of-war between what we hoped to grow and what we were *told* would grow. If farming had a soundtrack that month, it would have been a mix of sighs, muttered complaints and the occasional, heroic attempt at optimism.

By then, we thought we'd already earned our stripes. Hadn't we wrestled our way through bureaucratic quicksand to get our names added to the 7/12 extract? Didn't we survive the Bull Run Incident, when a gang of opportunistic bovines gorged themselves on our carefully planted crops? Even the electric pole saga—complete with village politics and negotiations that felt straight out of a gangster film—had ended in our favour. But those challenges, as it turned out, were just the warm-up. The true headliner was the daily chorus of 'Won't grow here.'

It didn't matter what we proposed—new crops, different techniques, even the occasional offbeat idea inspired by a YouTube farming channel. The answer was always the same, delivered with unshakeable certainty: 'Won't grow here.' It wasn't just an opinion; it was treated like a universal truth, etched into the very soil.

Take the time I showed up with a pouch of black turmeric seeds and two prized blue banana saplings. I felt like a modern-day agricultural pioneer, certain I was about to revolutionise farming in Raigad. Grim Sanjay—our resident sceptic and self-appointed guardian of tradition—stared at the saplings as if I'd just handed him a pair of alien artefacts.

'These won't grow here,' he declared, his tone as final as a concrete boundary wall.

'Why not?' I asked, determined to maintain my enthusiasm.

'Foreign trees don't work here,' he replied, as though Maharashtra's soil had some kind of nationalist agenda.

Undeterred, we planted the blue bananas in a corner of the farm that was as remote as it was symbolic—akin to exiled royalty awaiting a comeback. The turmeric seeds, too, were sown with a mixture of hope and defiance, though I could feel Sanjay's scepticism hovering over the field like a stubborn cloud.

Suzann's attempts to innovate weren't spared either. When she suggested planting avocados, Sanjay reacted as though she'd proposed setting fire to the farm. 'Avocados don't grow here,' he said, his voice laced with the kind of disdain usually reserved for brash city folk who didn't know their cashews from their chikoos.

It wasn't just ambitious crops that got hit with the dreaded 'won't grow' decree. Even something as straightforward as jowar (sorghum) was met with the same resistance. Every conversation followed a maddeningly predictable script:

'Can we plant jowar?'

'No.'

'Why not?'

'It doesn't grow here.'

'Has anyone tried?'

'No, because it won't grow.'

'And how do we know that?'

'Because no one plants it.'

It was a dizzying cycle, a song stuck on repeat, and we were slowly losing our patience. Yes, we were farming novices. Yes, we were two Bandra girls who didn't know the first thing about soil quality or irrigation. But the idea that nothing new could be tried was enough to make us dig in our heels—and dig them in deep.

We decided to stop arguing and start experimenting. If the farm was determined to resist us, we would resist right back. We began with nachni (finger millet), varia (barnyard millet) and wheat—crops Sanjay had all but written off as hopeless. To his great surprise (and perhaps ours), they thrived. Emboldened, we expanded our repertoire to include sweetcorn, tomatoes, chillies, aubergines and watermelons.

The sweetcorn was our first unambiguous victory. Twenty plump, golden ears emerged from the fields, so sweet they tasted like dessert straight from the stalk. Even Sanjay, grudgingly, admitted they were impressive—though not without a complaint about how much water they'd used.

The watermelons were a mix of triumph and timing. Half of them were glorious: juicy, red and sweet enough to make us forget the heat, even if just for a moment. The other half, however, fell victim to an overzealous early harvest, their pale interiors tasting more like cucumbers suffering from identity crises. Still, we counted this as a win—the problem wasn't the watermelons themselves but our impatience. A lesson learnt, and one we were determined to correct the next time around.

The bajra, meanwhile, had been growing beautifully—until one fateful night when a flock of avian bandits descended. By morning, the once-thriving field had been stripped bare, the stalks standing forlorn like silent witnesses to a crime.

Even with mixed results, we saw these experiments as victories. Crops no one believed could grow here were proving otherwise, one stubborn sprout at a time. Even the chillis turned out decently, and Sunil made a fiery Maharashtrian-style pickle using a recipe passed down through his family for generations. We bottled it, distributed it to friends and family, and sent any contributions straight to support the kids in the local hamlet. The aubergines, though modest in number, found their purpose—they were pickled and added to the line-up of farm-made delights.

In the previous chapter, I told the story of our bountiful tomato harvest and how it became jar after jar of marinara sauce. The real stars of that episode, however, were the tomatoes themselves—bright red, misshapen and bursting with flavour. Bottled under the 'Two Bandra Girls' label, the sauce was met with rave reviews from friends and family, and we were briefly hailed as culinary mavens and tomato whisperers. Sanjay, true to form, remained unimpressed. 'Too much effort,' he muttered. 'You should stick to mango and cashew.' And that, really, was the crux of it. For all our small successes, Grim Sanjay remained steadfast in his belief that we were wasting our time experimenting with new crops. 'Why not just stick to what works?' he argued.

But by this point, we were well past doing only what tradition approved of. We were determined to make the farm ours, in every sense of the word. And so, the battle of wills continued.

Then, out of nowhere, Sanjay dropped his latest bombshell: 'The real problem is water pressure.' He said it with the air of someone delivering a revelation, though the issue had clearly been simmering in the background for months.

'Has the water table dropped?' we asked, trying to stay calm.

'No.'

'Are the pumps broken?'

'No.'

'Is there a blockage?'

'No,' he repeated, shaking his head as if we were the ones being unreasonable.

Then the missing link snapped into focus.

Thanks to the Government Survey—the Great Boundary Drama—we had discovered that a large stretch of land at the highest elevation was actually ours.

Lovely news. Until we tried to farm it.

Our two pumps, loyal but not heroic, simply could not push water up to that new upper field. The moment we tried irrigating it, the pressure collapsed. The lower fields got nothing. The upper field got even less. The entire system behaved exactly like we felt—overheated, overwhelmed and utterly out of patience.

So the problem wasn't underground magic. It was physics.

Boring, stubborn physics.

And in that heat, with tempers rising and pressure falling, the only solution we could think of—our most Bandra-meets-Raigad instinctive response—was simple:

Borewell Number Three.

Which meant, inevitably, that our next chapter began not with machinery or measurements, but with a barefoot man and a coconut.

21

Of Dowsers, Dry Wells and Coconuts

May 2023

WHEN WE FINALLY DECIDED TO CALL THE DOWSER, IT wasn't out of belief or tradition—it was out of sheer, sun-baked desperation.

Everyone had an opinion. Everyone had a warning. Everyone had a theory. And when the theories finally tired themselves out, someone muttered the inevitable: 'Bring the coconut man.'

And honestly, calling the dowser felt like instinct. After all, he had been our first real taste of farm magic. Back in Year One, Mahesh had arranged for a dowser—a man who claimed he could locate underground water armed with nothing more than a coconut. It was part science, part sorcery, and entirely mesmerising. Mahesh swore by him. 'The coconut,' he had insisted, wide-eyed, 'stood up by itself.'

This marvel had happened twice, and both times we had drilled with the confidence of people who believed the universe was finally on their side. And twice, at fifty feet, water had gushed forth with theatrical flourish, as if the land itself had decided to reward our efforts. It had felt like magic, and for a while, we smugly believed we had conquered the farm's thirst.

So yes—by the time Year Three's water crisis arrived, the coconut had already earned our loyalty.

But Sunil—invigorated by exactly one YouTube tutorial on groundwater mapping—suggested we try 'a more scientific approach'. A proper hydrologist. Instruments. Satellite readings. Soil conductivity. A bill for ₹26,000.

We considered it for all of three seconds. Then remembered the dowser cost ₹1,200. That he had a 100 per cent success rate. And that we were, at heart, self-styled garib shetkaris (poor farmers—at least in our imagination).

Decision made.

The dowser arrived with quiet confidence, dressed in well-worn grey trousers, a black T-shirt and mud-streaked brown shoes. He carried no maps, no instruments—just a lone, slightly shrivelled coconut, looking every bit like a weary veteran of the water-finding wars. He cradled it with the reverence of a master craftsman, murmuring something under his breath. A blessing? A negotiation? Or perhaps a gentle plea for cooperation? At this point, we were placing more faith in a coconut than in modern science.

What could possibly go wrong?

Balancing the coconut on his open palm, he began to walk. We held our breath. Unbelievably, the coconut wobbled—our hopes soared—then it stilled. The dowser frowned. We frowned. He moved on.

After what felt like an eternity of nail-biting anticipation, the coconut finally stirred. First, a hesitant wobble. Then, a slight tremor. And just when we thought it was all an elaborate hoax, it suddenly quivered with purpose, like an over-caffeinated squirrel deciding to bolt. Then, dramatically, it stood upright, as if delivering the final verdict of an ancient oracle.

'There,' the dowser announced.

'There?' Suzann repeated, peering at the spot. It was in the lowest part of the farm, comically close to our first borewell. Unless we planned on building an aqueduct or training pigeons to deliver water, it was useless.

'Can you ... try again?' Sunil asked, in his best we're-desperate-but-trying-to-be-polite tone.

The dowser sighed and resumed his march, coconut cupped reverently. It did nothing. It remained limp. We could almost hear it yawning. Then, suddenly, it perked up—right on the very edge of the ravine.

This was the same ravine we had spent two years treating with the wary respect one normally reserves for live wires and unpredictable relatives. The land here sloped dramatically—nearly fifty metres from its highest point to its lowest—and that corner in particular was a menace. Come monsoon, the waters from the Sahyadri mountains gush down this part of our farm and transform that innocent-looking dip into a roaring, untamed waterway, the kind that thinks nothing of dragging off rocks, branches and, once, a very alarmed-looking goat.

So when the coconut chose *that* spot, my response was immediate. 'Absolutely not,' I declared. 'One monsoon and that borewell will be at the bottom of the valley.'

'Can you try somewhere higher?' Suzann asked, arms crossed. The dowser sighed again, in the way one sighs at children asking why the sky isn't green.

Meanwhile, Sunil and Maruti decided to take matters into their own hands. Sunil, holding his own coconut with the determination of a Jedi attempting telekinesis, got nothing. His coconut remained resolutely limp, refusing to so much as twitch. Maruti, on the other hand, ran around wildly, waving his coconut like a wand, announcing water sources with reckless enthusiasm. At one point, he triumphantly declared water under Sunil's shoe.

'Congratulations,' Suzann said. 'You've struck foot moisture.'

The dowser, ever the consummate professional, ignored them entirely. He moved methodically across the field, adjusting his grip, waiting for the coconut to react. We watched, half-hopeful, half-resigned to the ridiculousness of it all.

Finally, he found another spot—one that, at last, was equidistant from both fields. This one actually made sense. We managed to persuade Maruti to put his energy to better use, marking the chosen location with a pile of stones.

Feeling emboldened, we led the dowser across the narrow road that bisects our farm and urged him to try one last time in the second field. He paced around with determination—though, judging by his quickened steps, he was just as eager to wrap things up before lunch.

Eventually, he paused, seemingly having found another promising spot. But then, for reasons known only to the mystical brotherhood of dowsers, he shook his head and dismissed it as a false positive.

'Wait, what? Why?' I asked.

He simply shrugged. 'Ignore it.'

And so we did. By this point, questioning the dowser's methods felt about as productive as debating milk prices with a cow.

After what felt like an eternity of coconut-watching, he finally returned to the one spot between the two fields that he had marked earlier. 'This is the only one,' he said with finality. The coconut had spoken, and there was no room for debate. Science had its sophisticated instruments, but faith operated on its own peculiar, unwavering logic.

We stood there, staring at the ground, as if sheer force of will might persuade an underground river to materialise beneath our feet. The dowser, his job done, dusted off his hands and looked at us expectantly.

Well, he said, as though awaiting applause.

We sighed. We had hoped for a miracle, but today, the coconut had rationed its magic.

A few days later, the drilling rig arrived—a smaller one this time, thank heavens—the kind that could navigate the Fiend Highway without snapping in half or requiring us to beg the neighbour for access again. It still managed to roar like an enraged bull though, utterly unimpressed by our coconut-based decision-making.

The drilling operator, a man who had likely seen more dry wells than successful ones, watched impassively as the drill chewed through layer after layer.

At 50 feet, nothing.

At 100 feet, still nothing.

By 150 feet, our optimism was running on fumes.

At 300 feet, the drilling operator cut the engines and climbed down. 'Dry,' he declared.

And just like that, the rig packed up, leaving behind a single lonely plastic pipe protruding from the earth—a solemn monument to our crushed hopes.

We stood in silence, staring at the empty borewell. Betrayed. Bamboozled. Hoodwinked by a hairy nut.

The borewell boss, ever the optimist, shrugged. 'Maybe the coconut's on vacation', he said.

'Or just holding out for a better drilling crew,' I muttered under my breath.

He didn't take offence; in fact, he chuckled. 'Wait a month,' he said. 'Drop a pebble down. Maybe you'll hear a splash.'

We had long abandoned any illusion of control and instead settled into the strange rhythm of farming—a delicate dance between optimism and sheer delusion.

The farm, unmoved by our latest round of crises, carried on as always. Rice season had returned again, water or no water. Paddy was indifferent to our borewells; it drank straight from the monsoon and grew with a confidence we envied. Our real worry lay beyond the rains, in the crops that depended on the water we didn't have—the winter sowing that would demand planning, pressure and some reliable way to irrigate the fields for which our existing borewell pressure simply wasn't sufficient.

And the failure of Borewell 3 had made one thing painfully clear: the solution wasn't hidden in the depths of the earth. It was in how we managed the water we already had.

That's when the idea of a storage tank took shape. Instead of pinning our hopes on yet another borewell, we would pump water from our existing ones into a large overhead tank, ensuring a steady, dependable supply even through the hottest, driest months. Sanjay, true to form, dismissed the plan with his usual doom-laden pronouncement: 'Such a thing has never been done.' But by now, we'd learnt to treat 'never been done' as a green light to forge ahead.

Plans were made, measurements taken and we marked out the space where the tank would rise—after the monsoon rains, of course. With every step forward, we could almost hear the tank promising what the third borewell couldn't: water, delivered not by coconut magic or drilling drama, but by plain, stubborn engineering.

And before we could catch our breath, June arrived—and with it, the quiet, complicated start of a new kharif season.

22

Kharif Planting Again

June 2023

JUNE ARRIVED ON THE HEELS OF THE FIRST TENTATIVE monsoon showers, and with it came the start of the kharif season—our annual reminder that farming, like life, restarts whether we're prepared or not. But this year, the hills around us felt oddly muted. Fields that once buzzed with the sounds of sowing lay still. All the neighbouring farmers had decided to skip paddy cultivation altogether; the erratic rains, rising labour costs and steady migration towards city jobs had nudged them towards caution rather than optimism.

Our fields, however, were stirring to life. Because this year, we were doing things differently.

During the last kharif season, we had relied entirely on Vishwas and his bull-drawn plough—a system built on equal parts hope, luck and the bull's mood that morning. Some days, the bull bounded forward with unexpected enthusiasm. Other days, it stood frozen like a statue, refusing to budge an inch. And Vishwas, though well-meaning, was not exactly a model of consistency. Whether he would show up, which tools he remembered to bring, or how long he planned to stay were all variables in an equation no one could quite solve.

So when Sunil's old school friend Dinesh gifted us a power tiller—a sturdy little machine that digs and turns the soil far faster than any bull ever could—it felt like stepping through a portal into a new era. This gleaming machine didn't wander off or need coaxing or negotiate like a bored bureaucrat. It simply got on with the job. Tasks that once took days of delicate pleading—with man and beast alike—now took a few steady passes across the field. Precision replaced chaos; efficiency replaced drama.

The power tiller arrived just in time to tackle the freshly terraced fields, transforming rocky soil into workable farmland with impressive ease. As it rolled across the land, churning the earth with mechanical precision, even Sanjay couldn't hide his reluctant admiration. It was a small but gratifying win—one less dependency, one more stride towards self-sufficiency.

With the groundwork laid, we fertilised the newly levelled paddy fields with tractor-loads of cow dung and prepared for sowing. Ambemohar, Indrayani and Assamese black rice were tucked into the soil, our hopeful trio, carrying our aspirations for a good kharif season.

And yet, for all its unpredictability, last year's had its own charm.

We missed the chatter drifting across the fields. The silly jokes traded between Vishwas's crew. The way he spoke to his bull as though it were an exasperating coworker—one who never checked messages and frequently ignored instructions.

We missed the lunches his wife packed in steel dabbas for everyone—bhakris, chicken curry, rice and that lemon pickle capable of reviving even the most frayed mood. We missed the midday break under the jamun tree, when the work paused but camaraderie thrived. We missed the soundtrack of neighbouring farms: songs wafting over the hills, laughter carrying across the valley, the warm rhythm of many hands working in unison.

This year, the silence was unmistakable.

Progress had arrived at the farm, but it had come without the familiar din of community. Ours was the only farm sowing for miles. No crews worked in the next field. No voices carried on the wind. No bull snorted its disapproval from a few terraces away. Just the steady hum of machinery and our tiny crew, heads down, getting things done.

As if on cue, the farm added one more unexpected delight.

The stray dog who had adopted us months earlier produced four plump, wriggling puppies. They zigzagged through the grass with reckless abandon, convinced they were essential members of the operations team. Their chaos filled the silence in a way that made the stillness easier to bear.

Standing amidst the fields—rice swaying, puppies tumbling underfoot—we felt something dangerously close to peace. It was tempting to believe, just for a moment, that things were finally aligning.

But beneath the green, beneath the laughter and the illusion of order, something else was stirring.

A shadow none of us recognised yet—quiet, insistent, and far more personal than anything the farm had thrown at us so far.

Soon, it wouldn't be the land that needed tending. It would be one of us.

23

A Health Crisis

August 2023

BY AUGUST, TWO YEARS OF HARD LESSONS WERE FINALLY beginning to show. The days unfolded with an almost reassuring predictability: seedlings getting sown on time, weeds behaving themselves, harvest plans looking less like guesswork and more like intention. For the first time, we allowed ourselves to believe we had found our footing.

Which is why the phone call hit like a cruel blow.

It was late in the evening when Maruti—the Imp, our indefatigable, endlessly cheerful right hand—rang. His voice, usually bright and bubbling with mischief, was thin. Fragile. He said he was breathless, too dizzy to stand. Something was wrong, he whispered.

Alarm bells rang instantly. Sanjay, always reliable in a crisis, was summoned and he whisked Maruti off to the nearest hospital—at midnight, no less.

Of course, 'nearest hospital' in rural Maharashtra is a phrase that deserves an asterisk. This wasn't a short drive on a smooth road with streetlights and signboards. No, it involved an eight-kilometre descent on a road Google Maps refused to acknowledge, another ten kilometres to the nearest town, and yet another twelve to a government hospital open at such an ungodly hour. Public transport? Forget it. The only thing rarer than a bus around here is rain in May.

So off they went, our Sanjay and ailing Maruti, navigating rural Maharashtra by moonlight. Hours later, the news came back: Maruti was kept in the delightfully bleak outpatient ward overnight, administered two bottles of saline, and pronounced fit for discharge by morning. Crisis averted. We breathed a collective sigh of relief, patted Maruti on the back with a few stern words about staying hydrated, and returned to the business of farming.

For a time, things seemed like they were back to normal. Maruti was back to climbing ladders, digging trenches and running circles around the rest of us, his usual boundless energy on full display. Until it wasn't.

Another call came, this time in the middle of the afternoon: Maruti reporting chest pain and stomach cramps. Sanjay, grumbling about his latest role as an impromptu paramedic, was once again dispatched to the rescue. This time, the doctors decided to dig a little deeper. Blood tests were run and ultrasound scans ordered, all while we received live updates courtesy of Sanjay, whose running commentary was equal parts helpful and panic-inducing.

A day later, the doctor prescribed the standard Indian medical trifecta: an antacid, a course of antibiotics and paracetamol. Yet, despite this treatment cocktail, Maruti's condition didn't improve. Each day brought new complaints—palpitations, fatigue and breathlessness. We begged him to rest and offered to hire additional help, but Maruti, ever stubborn, refused to sit idle. As his health declined, I decided it was time to escalate matters. Armed with all his medical reports, I turned to our trusted Bandra-based 'Doc-to-the-Stars', Dr Hingorani. Though accustomed to treating celebrities, he was unfailingly kind to everyone.

He took one look at the reports and frowned. 'There's a chance this is intestinal tuberculosis,' he said.

And just like that, panic set in.

Intestinal TB. The words alone were enough to send me into a spiral of logistical chaos. Could we get him admitted to a Mumbai hospital? How would we manage the farm in his absence? Mahesh, our manager and man-about-town who somehow knows everyone worth knowing, stepped in like a knight in slightly dusty armour. Having worked with NGOs in the area, he reassured us that the state government's approach to TB treatment was not only effective but free. If Maruti tested positive, he'd receive full treatment at no cost, and his family would also be tested and cared for.

Armed with this information, Mahesh and Maruti set off for the nearest Public Health Centre, where tests were conducted with admirable efficiency. Updates poured in—photos of Maruti on a gurney, being wheeled in for a CT scan—and after what felt like an eternity, the results arrived. The scan was clear. No TB.

As a precaution, and before the final report was formally confirmed, the government doctor handed over a complete course of TB medication, along with clear instructions on dosage, timing and what to watch out for. The thoroughness was impressive, especially given that every test, scan and medicine was provided free of charge. But the tension didn't ease. Vandana, Maruti's wife was inconsolable, his sister called daily with dire stories of relatives lost to TB, and Maruti himself was a constant source of updates on his health.

At the advice of the Public Health Centre, we opted for the more conclusive TB antigen gold test. The wait was agonising, but when the results came in, relief washed over us: negative. No tuberculosis.

Still unconvinced, Dr Hingorani ordered additional tests to rule out other abdominal issues. This meant that poor Maruti, already worn out from the ordeal, had to shuttle back and forth between the farm and the government hospital. One of the tests required fasting, but in true Maruti fashion, he had enthusiastically polished off a hearty breakfast before his first appointment, turning what should have been a straightforward visit into multiple trips. In the end, however, the final reports were unequivocal: no tuberculosis of any kind, no abdominal issues, nothing alarming.

The final diagnosis? Indeterminate but manageable. Doc prescribed a regime of lifestyle changes—less spice, less oil, more protein and a generous helping of fruits and vegetables. Maruti's diet underwent a dramatic overhaul; apples and eggs became his new daily staples, while his wife, under strict instructions, toned down the heat in her cooking.

Months have passed without incident, and we remain cautiously optimistic. Looking back, what stood out most wasn't just Maruti's resilience or Grim Sanjay's midnight vigils or Mahesh's unflinching support, but the surprising efficiency of the rural healthcare system. The doctors were experienced, compassionate and incredibly thorough. In a country where government services are often the punchline of a bad joke, this was a rare moment of pride.

Who knew that one of the most reassuring things about farming in rural Maharashtra wouldn't be the soil or the rain—but the healthcare?

24

Wild Encounters

Mid-August–September 2023

Mid-August to September is a strange stretch in the farming calendar. The weeks between sowing our paddy fields and harvesting the rice feel like an overlong monsoon—heavy with anticipation and very little action. There isn't much for us to do besides the occasional weeding, chasing off overconfident mice, and standing around watching the rice grow like anxious parents at a school play, silently praying their child remembers all their lines. If you've never been near a paddy field just as the kernels begin to show, you should—it smells like nature's own brand of fine perfume, a heady blend of earth, water and life itself. The scent feels ancient, something our ancestors would have recognised as both promise and reward.

While the monsoon cloaks the farm in fifty spectacular shades of green, draping the hills in mist and filling the air with crickets and frogs performing enthusiastic nightly concerts, it simultaneously declares open season on the roads. Our weekly journeys turn into tyre-thumping endurance trials that demand the emotional preparedness of an extreme sport and an unshakeable faith in suspension systems. We brace for impact, pray the tyres hold and swear steadily at every fresh crater, all while pretending this is an immersive, character-building introduction to the 'authentic rural experience'. It is truly the best of times and the worst of times.

And then, just as our spines consider early retirement, the farm reveals itself—lush, alive, impossibly beautiful and entirely indifferent to the inconvenience it takes to reach it. A place that gives generously in spectacle while remaining stubbornly unmoved by our need for ease.

That year, the farm had an unexpected parade of visitors, each one keeping us on our toes.

One such surprise visitor awaited us in mid-August when we arrived to find Maruti and his wife Vandana stomping around the farm perimeter in gumboots. This was shocking because we had spent the best part of two years trying to persuade them to wear wellies in the wet fields, only for them to treat the boots as museum artefacts. And now, here they were, properly booted up, looking more prepared than we ever had been.

Before we could even get out of the car, Vandana came sloshing towards us, waving frantically.

'Jaldi ghala!' she commanded, holding out wellies for us to don.

Mildly alarmed but obedient, we struggled into them before asking what was going on.

'Ajgar ahe, madam,' Maruti announced gravely, pointing towards our nachni field.

'Ajgar?' My brain immediately conjured up images of a crocodile, an enormous reptile sunning itself menacingly in our fields. But how? There wasn't a water body for miles! A barrage of increasingly ridiculous questions followed—how did it get here? Had it walked? Had it hitched a ride on a bullock cart? And most importantly, why on earth did they think rubber boots would be any help against a crocodile?

Suzann, watching my growing panic, sighed. 'Why do you think an ajgar needs water?'

And that's when it dawned on me—my Marathi had betrayed me yet again! Ajgar wasn't a crocodile, as I had imagined, but a python. A crocodile was a magar.

And not just any python—a very large, very pregnant one, now comfortably settled in our nachni field, presumably preparing to introduce a swarm of baby serpents into the world.

Maruti declared the field off-limits and insisted we observe from behind the fence. Never mind that a python could glide through the barbed wire as easily as a knife through butter—we humoured him and spent an absurd amount of time peering into the field from various angles. Naturally, we saw nothing.

'I swear she's there,' Maruti insisted. 'When I walked past earlier, she lifted her head—hissed at me.'

'That's funny,' Sunil mused, deadpan. 'That's exactly what Arti does when I ask if there's more coffee.'

Our go-to naturalist friend, Surya, advised us to leave her alone—she would slither off in her own time. The forest department said the same, but offered to relocate her if she overstayed her welcome. We decided to give her some space.

Two weeks later, we returned to check on our rice, only to find ourselves the reluctant centre of village gossip.

As we drove past the neighbouring hamlet, we noticed people whispering and pointing at us with the intensity usually reserved for soap opera villains. Something was up. Bracing ourselves for the worst (possibly the return of the Farm Fiend), we sped to the farm and looked around—everything seemed fine.

We asked Maruti for an update on Ms Python. That's when Maruti nearly exploded with excitement.

'Forget the python! She's gone,' he practically shouted. 'A tigress was on the farm last night!'

A tigress. On our farm?

We laughed. This had to be a case of mistaken identity—there had never been a tiger sighting in our area. Surely it was just a leopard?

'No, no. Vaag,' Maruti insisted, using the Marathi word for tiger. Not just a tiger, but a tigress. With three cubs.

Sunil, ever the sceptic, muttered, 'It was probably just the local Shiv Sena branch head prowling around.'

(By way of explanation, the Shiv Sena's symbol is a tiger. This joke, however, did not land well. Maruti looked deeply offended, as if we had insulted his eyesight as well as his ancestors.)

By now, a small crowd had gathered, eager to corroborate the tale. Apparently, Madam Tigress and her cubs had taken a leisurely evening stroll through the village behind our farm before strutting onto our land. She had paused, surveyed her audience, then let out a mighty roar—sending Maruti and his cohorts into near cardiac arrest—before meandering off towards the abandoned municipal hospital two kilometres away.

There, under the shade of a tree, she had spent the rest of the night—unbothered, unhurried and completely indifferent to the chaos she had left in her wake.

For the next ten days, the farm was abuzz with tiger fever. Sightings, stories and theories poured in from all directions. Grim Sanjay knew someone who knew someone who had a photo of her and the cubs. Mahesh called to say she had feasted on some goats and a buffalo. Every conversation somehow led back to Madam Tigress. Our neighbours, usually unfazed by most wildlife encounters, spoke of her in hushed, reverent tones, as though she were some celestial being who had deigned to visit us. Even the forest department became involved, sending a team to confirm the sighting and monitor her movements.

At first, the knowledge that a tigress had been prowling around our farm was thrilling. We found ourselves scanning the ground for paw prints, half-hoping and half-dreading to find one. Sunil and Suzann debated setting up camera traps, but the villagers vetoed the idea—no one wanted a reminder that the queen of the jungle had wandered so close to their homes. More than once, we half-joked about setting up a ticket counter at the farm gate and charging visitors to see wildlife, since farming certainly wasn't paying the bills.

Suzann, ever the realist, leaned against the toolshed and sighed. 'So, let me get this straight,' she said. 'First, we had a gigantic, possibly hormonal python setting up a maternity ward in our field. And now, we've got a literal queen of the jungle prowling through our farm like she owns the place?'

'Sounds about right,' I said.

'And we still haven't managed to scare off those mice?'

Maruti, who had been listening, looked deeply hurt. 'Madam, mice are very clever.'

Then, just as suddenly as she had arrived, Madam Tigress vanished into the forest. Gradually, the whispers of fresh sightings stopped. The forest department declared she had likely moved on to a more secluded area, away from human habitation. The villagers, relieved, returned to their daily routines, and our farm, after a brief stint as the most exciting place in the district, was once again just a farm.

But something had changed. Every now and then, Maruti stopped in the middle of a task, glancing towards the treeline as though expecting her to reappear. Vandana took to clapping her hands loudly when walking alone, just in case. Even we found ourselves stepping a little more cautiously, attuned to every rustle in the undergrowth. The mice, of course, remained completely unbothered by all of this and continued their reign of terror in our rice fields, utterly convinced they were the true apex predators on the farm.

After an eventful month of pythons and prowling queens, farm life settled back into its usual rhythm. The rice continued to grow, the mice continued their mischief, and we went back to watching over our fields, wondering what unexpected visitor might show up next. Given our track record, we figured it was only a matter of time before a bear strolled in, took one look at us and decided to file for squatter's rights.

25

Kharif Harvest—Black and White

November 2023

As WE STOOD AMID THE FIELDS AFTER LAST YEAR'S DISMAL harvest, the view before us felt almost unreal. Fresh green stalks swayed in the afternoon breeze, moving with the kind of quiet confidence we hadn't seen in a long time. It was as though the land, after testing us through every possible challenge, was finally extending a small olive branch. The farm had a talent for pushing our limits. It questioned our decisions, mocked our optimism and seemed determined to find new ways to trip us up—whether through the relentless chorus of 'won't grow here', the Farm Fiend's well-timed interference or the sheer unpredictability of the seasons. And yet, every stubborn seedling, every tiny sprout, felt like it pushed back on our behalf.

Now, rows of Indrayani, Ambemohar and black rice stood proudly in neat formations, their glossy leaves shimmering under the midday sun. Nearby, patches of nachni (ragi/finger millet) and varai (sama/barnyard millet) added their own vibrant hues to the scene—a patchwork quilt of life and determination stitched together by our stubborn will. Each plant felt like a victory, a quiet defiance against all those who said it couldn't be done. The yield, we knew, wouldn't come close to the hundreds of quintals Vishwas, in his boundless optimism, had once predicted. But the sight of the fields thriving after months of uncertainty was enough to make every backache, sunburn and sleepless night worth it. With an estimated harvest of eighty to ninety kilos per rice variety, it wasn't grandeur—it was grit. And every grain felt like a hard-earned trophy.

When harvest season arrived, it was greeted with the kind of anticipation usually reserved for a long-awaited festival or the release of a blockbuster film. The Indrayani, with its slightly sticky grains known for their heavenly aroma, was the first to be picked. As we cut and gathered the rice into tight bundles, the golden husks sparkled in the sunlight like tiny jewels. Then came the black rice, with its deep, mysterious sheen that seemed almost too beautiful to eat. The varai, light, airy and delicate, followed—its stalks rustling softly in the breeze. Finally, the Ambemohar was brought in, its short grains exuding a fragrance that seemed to infuse the air itself, was brought in, transforming even the most mundane chore into a sensory experience.

With the fields delivering their bounty, Suzann and I began dreaming big. We envisioned Diwali hampers bursting with rustic charm: rice varieties nestled in brown paper, freshly milled nachni flour and nutty varai in clear pouches tied with earthy twine. They would be distributed through our social media channels, each hamper carefully curated to celebrate our hard work and share with others a tangible piece of the farm's heart. Every packet of nachni flour, every pouch of rice and every piece of twine would carry a story of resilience and connection to the land. Contributions would go towards supporting the neighbouring Adivasi hamlet, funding educational activities, recreational supplies and community events for the children, whose laughter had become a cherished constant, weaving warmth and joy into even the hardest days.

But, as we'd soon discover, sometimes it only takes one careless moment to unravel an entire season. The first blow came when our prized black rice was taken to the mill for threshing. What ought to have been a straightforward task ended in catastrophe. Grim Sanjay and sprightly Maruti returned, their faces etched with disbelief. The workers at the mill, in their carelessness, hadn't cleaned the rollers after threshing the previous batch of white rice. Our carefully cultivated black rice had been irreparably contaminated—fifteen kilos of white rice now mingled among its dark elegance, like unwelcome guests at an exclusive gathering.

When we opened the sacks the next morning, the sight was heartbreaking. The white grains stood out against the deep purple-black like a cruel joke, scattered as though mocking us. With Diwali fast approaching, separating about them in time for our hampers was impossible. It would take an army of hands and endless hours, neither of which we could afford during the festive season.

Months later, after painstaking labour and many resigned sighs, we managed to salvage forty kilos of black rice. By then, Diwali had passed, and our hampers had become a bittersweet memory of what might have been.

As if that weren't enough, nature too decided to remind us who was truly in charge. Just as the varai was harvested and laid out to dry, unseasonal clouds gathered ominously. The rains came suddenly, heavy and unrelenting, drenching the grains in minutes. Maruti and his family raced against the downpour, struggling to cover the harvest with tarpaulin while fending off an opportunistic army of mice, whose beady eyes glinted with mischief. The scene was almost farcical: buckets of rain, frantic humans and tiny predators darting in and out of the chaos, nibbling wherever they could.

Meanwhile, the Ambemohar was rushed to the same rice mill, leaving us to hope and pray it wouldn't meet the same fate as the black rice.

Back at the farm, the nachni too lay exposed on tarpaulins, its future hanging in the balance. Maruti, armed with nothing more than a broom and fierce determination, stood guard like a lone sentinel, swatting at every rustle and shadow in the grass. His family formed an impromptu defence line, their shouts echoing as they battled both mice and time.

Despite the setbacks, small victories emerged. The Ambemohar returned unscathed, its fragrant grains a reminder that not everything had gone wrong. The Indrayani, as always, was a star at the table, requiring nothing more than a drizzle of ghee and a sprinkle of salt to transform it into pure comfort. The nachni was eventually milled, its hearty flour finding its way into nourishing winter meals.

The black rice, however, remained a sore spot, a lingering reminder of what could have been. Determined to avoid such a disaster again, we resolved to take next year's harvest to a smaller, more meticulous mill run by Sanjay's uncle, even if it meant enduring a two-hour drive and higher transport costs.

Amidst the glow of hard-won victories and the sting of our own missteps, a sobering awareness returned—one we had first felt during sowing but which now settled around us with far greater weight. In the last two years, we had seen a big change come to the area. With none of our neighbours sowing paddy that season, our little patch of green stood alone, brave, stubborn or perhaps a little foolish, one of the only farms for miles still planting and harvesting rice. It was a peculiar kind of solitude, one that made us wonder whether we were pushing back against the odds or holding on to a version of farming the world around us had quietly begun to leave behind. The silent fields seemed witnesses to a profound shift, their emptiness carrying the weight of unspoken stories. Each day in this landscape taught us hard lessons of patience, perseverance and the fragile balance between hope and practicality.

And yet, in the stillness of the evening, a flicker of resolve took hold. The land, indifferent yet enduring, seemed to whisper that some battles were worth fighting—not just for the harvest, but for the stories that had taken root deep in the soil. We made an unspoken promise that evening: to keep going, not just for ourselves, but because we believed that our small patch of green still meant something. In the silence of the fields, our resolve grew. We would keep planting, keep harvesting and keep believing that the stories of the land deserved to be written—and lived.

YEAR FOUR: EARLY 2024

26

Boar-ed

May 2024

By our fourth year at the farm, May had stopped behaving like a month and started performing like a full-blown opera, complete with crescendos of chaos and unexpected interludes of quiet.

It's the time when the land demands attention, and we, like artists in a rural drama, rise to the challenge. The days stretch endlessly, the sun blazing like a vengeful god as we plough, fertilise and rid the fields of last season's leftovers. Think of it as spring cleaning, but instead of dust bunnies and forgotten socks, we're wrestling with stubborn stubble and rogue weeds.

The hum of the brush cutter provides a steady background rhythm, punctuated by the occasional clang of tools and an inventive repertoire of curses from Grim Sanjay and Maruti. The earthy scent of freshly turned soil hangs heavy in the air, mingling with the sweet-and-sour aroma of sweat and effort. We take deep breaths of it—because farm life offers a connection to the land that's as visceral as it is aromatic.

One thing you won't find here is stubble burning. That particular shortcut, with its apocalyptic smog and lung-clogging haze, isn't part of our repertoire. If farming is a relay race, then we've decided to run it the hard way, baton of sustainability firmly in hand. Sure, we're often left gasping for air, but at least the air we're gasping for is clean.

While Sanjay and Maruti sweat it out in the fields, I handle another battlefield entirely: procurement. Armed with nothing but a smartphone and sheer force of will, I spend hours on the phone with agro-suppliers and farmers across the country, negotiating prices, haggling over delivery timelines and generally doing my best impression of a stock market trader—except the commodities here are organic fertilisers and rice seeds. It's a game of high stakes and even higher patience. One misstep, and I could end up with substandard seeds or an empty wallet.

When the first of my meticulously sourced orders arrived, I tore open the boxes like a child on Diwali morning. Inside were treasures of the agricultural kind—rice seeds with the promise of bountiful harvests, turmeric roots exuding an aroma that belonged in a masala box and bags of agro-nutrients that might as well have been gold dust. But, as with everything on the farm, triumph is fleeting. My crowning glory, a one-tonne order of organic fertilisers, hit a logistical wall. No courier service wanted to touch it, and the prospect of driving to Nashik to retrieve it myself felt about as appealing as ploughing a field by hand.

Enter Sunil, my Marathi-speaking saviour. With effortless charm and a calm I could only aspire to, he coaxed the reluctant supplier into arranging a tempo delivery. When that blessed vehicle finally rumbled into Mumbai, packed to the brim with our precious cargo, I greeted it with the kind of reverence most people reserve for their first car. We got to work immediately: the farm car was filled with fertilisers, Sunil's sparkling sedan with seeds and a third batch was tucked away for delivery at a later date. It was a full-blown operation taking place in the building compound, complete with onlookers, spilled rice seeds and the faint aroma of neem-coated ambition.

The journey to the farm was a test of nerves. Every pothole felt like a personal affront, every sharp turn a potential disaster. I muttered silent prayers for the tyres and, by some miracle, we arrived at the farm unscathed. But as we rolled in, the usual excitement Sanjay and Maruti exhibited was conspicuously absent. Instead, they stood in the distance, shoulders slumped, as though mourning a great loss.

Sanjay approached, his face grim even by his own dour standards. 'Wild boars,' he said, the words carrying the weight of an epic tragedy. My heart sank, even as my mind raced to assess the damage.

We followed him to the banana field, each step heavier than the last. What awaited us was nothing short of devastation. Over fifty banana trees, once proud, green and six-foot-tall, lay in a broken, tangled heap. The field resembled a battlefield after a particularly vicious skirmish—trunks snapped into splinters, shredded leaves strewn everywhere, confetti from a party no one wanted to attend. These were the very same banana plants we had planted two years ago, right after the infamous Bull Run.

Maruti pointed to the evidence: coarse tufts of boar hair caught in the barbed wire and deep pug marks in the soft earth. The culprits? A sounder of ten wild boars—nocturnal hooligans with a penchant for destruction. These weren't your garden-variety pigs; these were the Hulk Hogans of the porcine world, each weighing up to 140 kilos and built like battering rams.

Wild boars, I've learnt, have a particular fondness for banana trees. They target saplings, gnawing on the tender bulbs. Then, as the bananas ripen, they shift their attention to the trunks, snapping them to access the fruit. A single boar can decimate up to ten trees in one night, and with ten of them on the rampage, it's game over.

It's no wonder that many farmers have begun to steer clear of cultivating crops like bananas near forested areas. But no one had warned us, and we were learning this harsh lesson through bitter experience.

As I stood amid the wreckage of what once was a thriving banana grove, I felt an unfamiliar weight settle over me. It wasn't just about the financial loss; it was the sting of helplessness, the realisation that no amount of planning could shield us from nature's whims. For all our optimism and effort, the land was reminding us of a truth it had known all along: farming is not a negotiation. It's a partnership with forces far beyond our control, one that requires humility, resilience and—on days like this—a lot of deep breaths. Sanjay suggested setting traps, though even he didn't look convinced. 'Khara sangu,' he sighed, 'jar janglee dukar sankatacha nirnay ghetla, dev suddha haat jodto.' (Truth be told, if a wild creature has decided on causing trouble, even God folds his hands in helplessness.)

We decided to replace the destroyed bananas with twenty Kesar mango trees, a move that felt less like a choice and more like an act of defiance. Still, with another field of thirty banana trees standing precariously close to the forest, the spectre of a second attack loomed large.

This incident was also a stark reminder of how fragile farming livelihoods can be. As we stood among the broken stalks, it became clear that this was not just about our bananas. It pointed to a larger system that leaves countless farmers stranded in moments like these. Unlike us, who could absorb the loss and pivot to planting a mango grove, an average small farmer might face devastation. A single night's destruction could wipe out an entire livelihood.

Curious about potential compensation, I called Mahesh to inquire about government aid. The news was predictably dismal: bananas, it turns out, cannot be insured in Maharashtra. Mangoes can be, but the claims process is so convoluted that Kafka would not just weep—he'd probably pen another novel about it.

In neighbouring Kerala, farmers can claim insurance for losses incurred due to wild elephants, but they have no such safety net against wild boars. It would be pointless to explore this issue state by state; it would only serve to deepen my despair as I realised the systemic failures within our agricultural support systems. Farmers are not even offered half the assistance they truly need.

And with each passing moment, it became increasingly clear that the devastation in our banana field was merely a symptom of a much larger problem. This wasn't just about wild boars or shattered trees, it was about the systemic neglect that left farmers vulnerable to forces far beyond their control. The absence of insurance for certain crops, the labyrinthine bureaucracy of claims processes, and the lack of effective support for wildlife conflicts painted a grim picture of a system straining at its seams.

The need for macro-level agricultural reforms feels urgent, pressing like the weight of an impending storm. Without meaningful changes—better insurance schemes, accessible compensation mechanisms and policies that acknowledge the real challenges of farming—more farmers will be forced to leave their fields, their livelihoods swallowed by a system that offers little in return.

This isn't just a farming crisis; it's an existential one. If the policies shaping our agricultural future continue to overlook these realities, we risk not only an agrarian collapse but also the erosion of the very fabric of rural life. The cracks are already visible, and the question isn't if but when they will widen into chasms.

I realised that what we were dealing with went beyond our own farm and spoke to a much wider reality of farming today.

Little did we know that while we were worrying about what was vanishing in Mahagaon, something entirely unexpected was about to stir in Mahure.

27

Are We Sitting on a Goldmine?

June 2024

WE HAD BARELY WRAPPED OUR HEADS AROUND THE bigger battle unfolding beyond our banana field when the universe, in its usual mischievous style, changed the subject.

The next plot twist came via phone. It was June 2024. Someone wanted to buy our Mahure land. A place that, until then, had been more daydream than farmland ... and now it had barged back into the conversation as though it had simply been waiting in the wings for its cue.

Mahure. Just the name was enough to send us spiralling into flashbacks.

A few months after we'd bought our first farm, Suzann and I, drunk on newfound confidence (or lunacy, depending on whom you ask), had decided to buy another piece of land. It was a mere seven kilometres away from our first farm. Seven kilometres! Practically next door, right?

Wrong. Those seven kilometres turned out to be more like a trek across dimensions. Our farm at Mahagaon was already something of a trial—a scrappy, untamed patch of weeds, rocks and thorny shrubbery that looked like Mother Nature's idea of a booby trap. This wild chaos sat uncomfortably close to a few city houses and a small Adivasi hamlet, making us feel like we were farming on the fault line between two worlds. We hacked, hoed and sweated like contestants in an endurance reality show, making friends (and maybe a few frenemies) along the way, until we finally wrangled a semblance of order from the anarchy.

But Mahure ... Mahure was something else entirely.

It was a postcard come to life: vast open fields framed by regal hills, a gurgling stream that looked handpicked by a Bollywood location scout, sunlight that fell in golden sheets over the landscape. It was the kind of place that made you want to plant your feet firmly, take a deep breath and proclaim, 'This is it! We'll grow roots here—literally and figuratively—and maybe, just maybe, write a masterpiece or two.'

Cue reality, barging in like an uninvited guest. Mahure was remote in a way that even the most rustic Instagram influencer wouldn't dare to hashtag. No electricity for miles, no mobile network, no neighbours—just us, the hills, a few trees and a silence so deep it was almost creepy. Seven kilometres? Try seven light-years.

Still, we had decided to semi-fence the place—a vague attempt at 'claiming' it—and left it to its picturesque solitude. We had even consulted our go-to rice guru, Vishwas, about its potential. He took one look, laughed until tears streamed down his face, and said, 'Rice? Here? Who's going to guard it? The monkeys? The birds?' He wasn't wrong. Mahure was practically a wildlife sanctuary, and anything we planted would likely end up in the bellies of local fauna before we could say 'harvest'. Without electricity or water supply, even building a shack for a farmhand was impossible. His advice was simple: 'Wait until civilisation gets here. Then maybe think about farming.'

So, we waited. And waited. Every few months, we'd take a break from wrangling weeds at Mahagaon to visit Mahure, sit by the stream and bask in the surreal joy of owning a slice of untouched wilderness. It became our personal postcard—lovely to look at, completely impractical to work on.

Which is why the phone call made no sense.

Someone wanted to buy our Mahure land. And they were offering a shockingly decent amount. Suzann and I scratched our heads, trying to figure out why anyone would pay good money for what we had dubbed 'Paradise Pointless'. We were just about to toast our unexpected windfall when—bam!—seven more offers rolled in. Seven! Suddenly, Mahure, which had been sitting quietly for years, was the hot new debutante of the real estate ball.

And then came the clincher: the Farm Fiend himself. The man had an uncanny ability to sniff out money like a bloodhound, and he wanted to 'help' us sell our 'useless' land, generously promising us a 'handsome profit'. Naturally, we were immediately suspicious. This was the same man who wouldn't loan you a bucket of water if you were on fire.

We decided to investigate, enlisting M&S (our trusted intelligence network, also known as the village gossip brigade). Their 'report' was a delightful mess of rumours—upcoming warehouses, industrial plans and the grand expansion of Dighi

Port. Mahure, our untouched Eden, was apparently poised to become the next big hub of industry. Our quaint paradise, it seemed, was no longer off the map.

Three years ago, Mahure had felt like the middle of nowhere, so remote it barely seemed real. Now, it was caught in the quiet buzz of transformation, suspended between its serene past and a lucrative future.

Had we been sitting on a goldmine all along? Perhaps. Or perhaps it had just taken a few seasons, a ripple of whispers and the right kind of ambition for the world to catch on. We thought we'd found a bit of paradise—but it turns out, it might just be paved with gold.

At the time of writing this, the offers haven't stopped. They arrive every few weeks—some earnest, some curious, some suspiciously enthusiastic. Meanwhile, several small concrete structures have begun sprouting across the neighbouring plots like mushrooms after rain. Rumour has it that compensation for land with a structure is higher than for a barren field.

The buzz continues. And for now, we're doing what farmers do best: waiting, watching and letting the land decide what happens next.

28

Vignettes from the Farm

LIFE ON THE FARM RARELY UNFOLDS IN GRAND NARRATIVES. It comes in fragments—small, vivid moments that don't demand full chapters but insist on being remembered. These are the stories shaped by chance encounters, peculiar traditions and the unpredictable moods of nature itself.

Some stories arrive quietly on foot, like the wandering barber who trades haircuts for sacks of peanuts and bottles of hooch, his scissors deftly snipping through both unruly hair and the latest village gossip. Others burst onto the scene in a clamour of activity—like the boar hunters who set off into the forest at dawn, armed with nothing more than lathis, a dash of bravado and an ample supply of illicit liquor, only to return empty-handed but brimming with the thrill of the chase.

Then there are those stories that tip the scales between the absurd and the sublime. Picture receiving an outlandish shopping list a couple of days before a farm visit—a quirky medley of requests that evolve from the practical to the downright ridiculous, ranging from spades and sickles to twenty-foot ladders and even the occasional bizarre pairing of toilet cleaner with a gun. Such lists are a ritual in themselves, a reminder that on this farm, the unexpected is always just a phone call away.

And amid all this lively chaos, quiet wonders still find their place. A pair of peacocks transforms the nachni fields into a private stage, their iridescent plumes catching the first light of day. Then, almost as if on cue, tiny red rain bugs—known locally as the 'miring'—emerge from the earth, their frantic scurrying a natural prophecy heralding the arrival of the monsoon with uncanny precision. Interwoven with these marvels is nature's own medicine cabinet: bhamburdi leaves to staunch a bleeding wound, the powdered bark of the Ain tree to soothe an upset stomach, and the pungent paste of the garlic creeper that works wonders on cuts and bruises.

These are the vignettes that shape our farm life—the small, fleeting moments that, when stitched together, form the essence of this place. They are stories without clear beginnings or endings, mere cycles repeated with the seasons, bound by the unyielding rhythms of land and life.

The Wandering Barber

The first time we saw a man whistling away on the narrow road that bisects our farm into unequal halves, we could only stare in amazement. He had a baseball cap worn backwards and a battered satchel slung over one shoulder. In his arms were two squawking chickens, their feet tied but their outrage unmistakable. A heavy sack of rice was strapped across his back, and balanced on his head was a straw basket, stuffed and teetering with the weight of village life.

Maruti hollered for him to stop and rushed over to speak with him. Curious, we wandered across. The man gently lowered the basket to the ground, revealing its contents: a child's rattle, a tangled heap of cotton sarees, cracked plastic mugs, a faded tin lunchbox and a small mountain of green chillies spilling from a torn newspaper cone.

Every third Sunday, just as the rooster's crow echoed across the hamlet, this figure would emerge on the horizon: the barber. It was a day set in stone. He left his home long before dawn and walked the length and breadth of Raigad, giving men their monthly shave and haircut. He had fixed dates for each collection of hamlets and villages and was eagerly awaited as the god of tresses and gossip. It was a job his father used to do before him, and his father before him. They were the family of Raigad Nais. With his battered satchel and a weathered cap, he was less a man and more a travelling institution. Unlike city barbers who dealt in cash and precision cuts, this man operated entirely on barter. In this informal, unpredictable system, services were exchanged for whatever his clients had to offer. The hamlet's men and boys of all ages lined up in various states of hair-related despair, eagerly awaiting their turn. Stories were shared and local gossip dissected with every snip of his scissors, with the occasional debate taking place about which village's hooch was truly superior. Maruti and his two boys were regular clients, and depending on what we were growing at that time, the barber was paid in watermelon, rice flour or with a sack of peanuts. Negotiations were fierce—the barber knew his worth. When he finally packed up and trudged to the next village, the hamlet's silence seemed louder, as if it too missed the lively banter of a haircut day.

Boar Hunters in High Spirits

Saturday mornings in the hamlet always begin with a ritual that, to outsiders, looks like the prelude to an epic war campaign. The men of the tribe, a ragtag battalion of self-proclaimed warriors, gather at dawn; their voices are hushed, but their excitement is unmistakable. The air smells of damp earth and wood smoke, and the sky, still tinged with the last shades of night, watches over their preparations for battle.

Armed with an assortment of weapons—lathis, sickles, the occasional rusting spearhead—they set off in search of their adversary: the wild boar. Their real weapon, however, is far from conventional. Bottles of potent hooch—the kind that can strip paint off a bullock cart and make a man forget he has a wife waiting at home—are passed around with solemn nods, as if they are drinking courage before a grand conquest.

With war cries loud enough to frighten every living creature within ten miles, they charge into the dense forest that borders our farm. A few of the younger men, high on bravado and hooch, wave to us as they run past, grinning and promising to bring us jars of boar pickle. But we never set our hopes on such gifts. For all the time we have been here, they have never once returned with a trophy wild boar.

Hours pass. The jungle echoes with their dramatic pursuits—one man tumbles into a muddy trench, another swears he locked eyes with the beast just before it vanished into thin air. The sun climbs higher, the heat presses down, but their spirits stay undeterred, fuelled by stubbornness and the occasional swig from an ever-dwindling bottle.

By noon, the great warriors return, emerging from the underbrush—mud-streaked, bruised and empty-handed, yet grinning like victorious conquerors. Grand tales of near captures fill the air, their stories swelling with every retelling. The boar, once an ordinary creature, grows larger with every word—its tusks longer, its hooves swifter, its cunning unmatched. By the time they reach the village square, it has become a monster the size of a temple elephant, an adversary so formidable it escapes only by divine intervention.

Their wives, unimpressed by yet another boarless hunt, greet them with folded arms and withering glares. The men, however, remain unfazed. The thrill of the chase is victory enough. The remaining hooch is shared in a final toast to their bravery, their laughter echoing into the night.

Perhaps next Saturday, they say, as the last drops vanish down their throats. The boar has only won this round.

Dancing Peacocks in the Nachni Patch

One crisp winter morning, when the air is still heavy with the scent of damp earth, the farm wakes to an unexpected spectacle. As the first rays of sunlight stretch over the fields, two peacocks step out from the brush, their feathers glistening like jewelled fans.

We stand frozen, our tools forgotten, as the performance unfolds before us. The birds move with regal grace, their iridescent plumes fanning out in an explosion of blues and greens. It is a courtship dance so mesmerising that Bollywood choreographers would throw in their towels in defeat.

The morning air fills with the rustle of feathers, the low hum of the wind and the distant calls of unseen birds. Time seems to slow, as if the entire farm pauses to witness this fleeting magic. And then, as suddenly as they appear, the peacocks vanish into the foliage, leaving behind only a whisper of movement and a lingering sense of wonder.

It is a moment so perfect, so surreal, that we could swear we have dreamed it.

Shopping Lists: The Outlandish Mumbai Farm Run

A couple of days before each farm visit, I call or text Grim Sanjay and Maruti, asking, 'Anything you need?' Over the years, their shopping lists have evolved from surprisingly practical to downright absurd, and sometimes to hilariously eccentric.

I still remember the time, early in the farm's first year, when Maruti sent me a terse message: 'Get pawda, koyta, and gamela.' I stared at my phone, muttering, 'Uh ... what?' A quick Google search cleared up the mystery—he was asking for spades, sickles and plastic tubs. For a moment, I wondered if there's a farmer's dictionary I should have read before all this began.

I called him immediately. 'Maruti, I live in Mumbai! Where am I supposed to find all this?' I demanded, half exasperated and half amused. His reply was calm as ever: 'It's Mumbai. I've been there once. Everything is available there!' And so began our wild treasure hunt through the winding streets of Bandra, ending in triumph at Khar market.

Our car would turn into a mobile warehouse, groaning under the weight of supplies, each time we barrelled off to the farm, every bump sounding like a cue in a slapstick comedy.

As time passed, the requests grew even stranger. One trip we picked up summer hats and torches; the next, a twenty-foot ladder—a ladder so absurdly long that squeezing it into the car had felt like cramming an elephant into a Mini Cooper. Vandana would often giggle over the phone before asking for jalebis or ladoos, as if she was ordering sweets for a royal feast.

Then came the day Sanjay dropped a line that sounded ripped from a bad spy novel: 'Get kulhads—make sure they have sharp blades.' I nearly spat out my coffee. The image of a razor-edged kulhad made my brain do a double-take. 'A sharp-bladed axe to you and me,' I muttered, half-awed, half-aghast.

What followed could be storyboarded: a furtive, full-blown covert operation with the air of an amateur heist. Word on the street—whispered like contraband—was that buying (or was it selling?) axe heads flirts with the edge of the law. It sat in a strange legal twilight none of us cared to explore. So we improvised secrecy.

We began in a cramped shop that smelled of oil and old paper, light leaking in through a dusty window. Shelves sagged with tools that had not seen daylight in a decade. We scanned every corner, fingertips brushing metal that promised mischief; when one axe head finally winked at us from behind a stack of tins, it felt like finding buried treasure. Each creak of a floorboard and shift of shadow turned ordinary retail into suspense cinema.

Prize in hand, we sprinted to the next stop for handles—thick, straight, honest wood that might survive a mango tree and a bad swing. Mumbai pressed down on us outside, with a heat that makes patience fray and shirts stick to backs. The axe head left to be sharpened, and the waiting felt cinematic—two extras in a high-stakes reel, sweating through our roles.

I couldn't help myself. 'How do I test sharpness?' I asked, half-laughing, half-terrified. 'Do I try a coconut?' The suggestion hung between us like a dare. When the axe head returned, gleaming and dangerous, we reassembled the thing with the exaggerated care of people handling something that could go viral for all the wrong reasons.

We parked as close to the shop as etiquette allowed, eyes flicking to every passerby. With furtive movements, we stowed the axes in the trunk; the dodgy seller leaned in and whispered, 'Don't speed—you might get stopped by the cops.'

We drove off with our loot, the car improbably heavy and our nerves taut. The idea of a police raid turned the whole escapade into a deliciously absurd thriller: equal parts menace and farce, a rural gadget run that played out like the climax of a spy caper—only funnier and entirely, gloriously ours.

There were also times when we hauled 100 metres of tarpaulin—squeezing us together like sardines in a tin—and enough strings and ropes to circle the globe. Yet nothing topped the bizarre request that arrived in a cryptic message: 'Get toilet cleaner and a gun.' I nearly dropped my phone as I read it. Taking a deep breath, I called Maruti for clarification.

'Toilet cleaner is running out,' he informed me, his tone carrying the usual impatience of someone who expected me to know already.

'But the gun?' I pressed, struggling to keep my tone light.

'Oh, that's to shoot the wild boars,' he replied as if discussing the weather forecast.

I protested, 'Maruti, I can't just go out and buy you a gun!'

His instant retort, 'Of course you can—you get everything in Mumbai. I've been there once,' left me shaking my head in disbelief.

Needless to say, that was one demand we had to refuse—a decision that was vindicated a few weeks later, when a sheepish Maruti admitted that his friend had been arrested for possessing an illegal gun.

Every trip to the farm became a madcap adventure—a mix of quirky shopping sprees, absurd conversations and more laughter than a comedy show. With every new list, I wondered what on earth I would be picking up next—and I couldn't help but laugh at the ridiculous, unpredictable joy of it all.

Red Bugs: The Harbingers of the Monsoon

Early June at the farm carries a certain stillness—a kind of expectant hush that hangs over the land like a held breath. The air is thick, humid and charged with the promise of rain, but the sky stays stubbornly clear, as if teasing the thirsty earth below. On one such visit, as we trudged through fields baked hard by the summer sun, we noticed something unusual.

Tiny flashes of red moved across the ground, darting with a frantic energy that felt out of place in the lazy heat. At first, we thought our eyes were playing tricks on us, but no—there they were, thousands of them, scurrying over the soil, vanishing as quickly as they appeared. They clambered over stones, darted between blades of grass and then, as if on cue, burrowed back into the earth, disappearing in the blink of an eye.

Maruti watched our confusion with the patience of a man long accustomed to city folk marvelling at the ordinary. Pointing at the tiny creatures, he declared with the certainty of a seasoned farmer, 'It will rain soon.'

We blinked at him. 'Because of ... the bugs?'

He nodded, perfectly serious. 'These are "miring". They come up only when the rain is about to arrive.'

Sceptical but curious, we turned to Google, our modern oracle. Sure enough, Maruti was right. Known as *roi ni* in Marathi, these little creatures were *Trombidiidae*—red velvet mites, or as they were poetically called, rain bugs. With their striking crimson hue, these eight-legged arachnids spend most of their lives hidden beneath the soil, emerging only when the humidity hits the perfect threshold, heralding the arrival of the monsoon.

And then, almost on cue, the first fat drops of rain splattered onto the dry, cracked earth. Within moments, the heavens opened up, unleashing a torrential downpour that sent us scurrying for shelter.

Maruti, unfazed, grinned. 'I told you.'

We watched as the dust melted into mud, the parched land greedily drank in the water and, somewhere beneath our feet, the miring had retreated, their brief prophecy fulfilled.

Nature's Pharmacy

Medicine on the farm doesn't always come in blister packs or brown bottles. More often, it grows wild—nestled in rock crevices, tangled in undergrowth or sprouting defiantly along well-worn footpaths. Its secrets are handed down like heirlooms, with remedies woven into daily life as naturally as the changing seasons.

Over the past three years, Grim Sanjay, Vandana and, most reliably, Maruti have pointed out all manner of scraggly creepers and stubborn shrubs, casually declaring their miraculous powers.

When I remember the names, I look them up. Sometimes I use Google Lens, which isn't always sure but tries its best.

Listed below are a few of the so-called cure-alls growing quietly across our land. I've included the Latin names where I could find them, but the rest is strictly hearsay, though no less fascinating for it.

Take bhamburdi (*Justicia procumbens*), for instance. It looks like nothing special, but in the hamlet, it's a first-aid essential. We saw it in action when Sunil had an unfortunate run-in with a particularly enthusiastic thorn bush. Blood was everywhere. Before we could so much as gasp, Maruti had calmly grabbed a fistful of bhamburdi, crushed the leaves in his hand, and slapped them onto the wound. The bleeding slowed almost immediately, as if the plant had taken offence and decided to fix things.

A few months later, at our first popti party, bhamburdi showed up again—this time tucked into the base of an earthen pot, flavouring the marinated chicken with its peppery bitterness and herbal mystery. Medicinal in more ways than one.

Then there's the wild banana plant (keliche jangli zad), whose dried powder is a longstanding cure for dog bites. I can practically picture Maruti's grandmother, pulling out a dented tin from a dusty shelf and mixing a bit into a paste while muttering something mildly alarming. With the number of strays in the area—not to mention our own ever-growing gang of four-legged freeloaders—it's easy to see why this remedy has endured.

For fevers that refuse to break, the women of the hamlet often turn to ranmare (*Celosia argentea*), commonly known as cockscomb or wool flower. According to Vandana, its pale, feathery blossoms are boiled into a dusky brew, served quietly and without fuss. She once watched a feverish child drink it slowly, propped against her mother's lap. By morning, her flush had faded, and she was chasing chickens again. No one celebrated; they simply nodded, as if the plant had done precisely what it was meant to do.

A particularly complex character in this cast of green healers is kallavi (*Gloriosa superba*), also known as the flame lily. Strikingly beautiful, with curling petals in shades of fire, it is as lethal as it is lovely. Every part of the plant is poisonous, especially the rhizomes, which contain high levels of the alkaloid colchicine. Ingested in the wrong dose, it can lead to nausea, seizures, organ failure and, in severe cases, death for both humans and animals. Accidental poisonings have occurred when the tubers have been mistaken for yams. More grimly, it has a history of deliberate misuse—in suicides, in murders, in whispered stories from both folklore and the front pages of newspapers. Yet, in tiny, controlled doses, kallavi has long been used in traditional medicine: to treat gout, ulcers, infertility and even snakebite. Some midwives still apply it topically to ease labour pain. However, this isn't a plant to experiment with. In India, its trade is illegal and punishable under the Poison Act. On our farm, it blooms near a shaded slope. We have learnt to admire it from a distance.

For an upset stomach, the bark of the ain tree (*Terminalia elliptica*) is dried and brewed into a dark, bitter decoction, strong enough to make even the most hardened farmer wince. It is not for the faint-hearted, but it does its job well, effectively curing indigestion, diarrhoea and stomach cramps in ways no over-the-counter syrup could ever hope to match.

A persistent cough calls for a steaming infusion of patharchur (*Bryophyllum pinnatum*) leaves. This plant grows abundantly along the edges of our fields, its thick, fleshy leaves rich in healing properties. When boiled into a robust tea and sweetened with a dash of jaggery, it serves as the go-to remedy for coughs, congestion and any bronchial infections caused by bacteria, a remedy favoured by village grandmothers who trust it far more than any store-bought lozenge.

Snakebites—mercifully rare, but not unheard of—are met with a swift application of naagvel (Piper betel) leaves, crushed and pressed against the wound, while an urgent prayer is offered to whoever might be listening. The logic of the treatment remains a mystery, but the faith behind it is absolute. Betel leaves—often called 'Green Gold'—have long played a role in traditional remedies, and modern studies are beginning to catch up. They may help with headaches, fungal infections, gastric ulcers and even wound healing, thanks to their cooling, antifungal, antioxidant and tissue-repair properties. Some early research suggests possible roles in managing diabetes, easing allergic reactions and relieving constipation. There's even talk of anti-cancer potential, though that remains firmly in the realm of lab studies.

And then there's panphuti (*Boerhavia diffusa*), the herb of choice when kidneys start sulking or water retention becomes a concern. It creeps low along the soil, easy to miss until you know what to look for. Locals swear by its detoxifying magic, whether in tea or paste form, and some even mix it into buttermilk for extra effect—though that particular preparation seems best left to the truly fearless.

For infected wounds, there is lasun vel (garlic creeper, *Mansoa alliacea*), its crushed roots and leaves forming a pungent paste that acts as a natural antibiotic. And then there is hirda (*Terminalia chebula*), its dried fruit ground into a fine powder and stirred into warm water to soothe sore throats and colds.

And since we're clearly the most on-trend farmers around (just ask our turmeric-stained hands and artisanal pickle labels), it only made sense that the land itself would follow suit. One afternoon, as we wandered past a wild, overgrown corner of the farm, Maruti pointed to a leafy plant and said, as casually as if discussing the weather, 'Sugar kami karayla changla ahe.'

I blinked. Was he suggesting the plant reduced sugar?

He nodded, chewing a twig with all the confidence of a village botanist. 'Lok khaatat. Blood sugar sathi.' Those with blood sugar eat it.

Out came Google Lens. A quick scan later, and there it was: *Costus igneus*, better known as the insulin plant. Native to Southeast Asia and widely used in Ayurvedic and traditional medicine, its leaves are said to help regulate blood sugar levels when chewed or brewed as tea. And it was growing wild on our land—completely uninvited, completely unbothered.

Roll over, Ozempic. Our weeds are doing the work now.

Out here, these plants aren't just a part of the landscape—they're a part of daily life. When a child scrapes a knee, when a farmer returns from the fields with a nasty gash, when the monsoon humidity brews yet another stubborn fever, the first instinct isn't to reach for a box of pills, but to turn to the land.

Because here, the earth still heals.

A note of caution here. With the exception of bhamburdi—which we've tested first-leg—consider this section a record of local knowledge, not medical advice. These remedies are rooted in tradition, not clinical trials, and while they're trusted by locals, they're not substitutes for professional care. For anything serious, see a doctor.

A Fine Line Between Brave and Crazy: A Field Guide for City Dwellers Turned Farmers

HERE'S THE HANDBOOK WE WISH SOMEONE HAD SLIPPED into our hands before we swapped sea-facing towers for silty fields. Not a how-to guide—more of a 'how-we-survived-it' guide. It's stitched together from bruised shins, misplaced optimism, and the occasional triumph. If you're a city dweller flirting with the idea of farming, consider this your preview of just how thin the line can be between bold and bonkers.

1. Choosing the Right Land is Everything

Our Experience:

We scouted endlessly, trekking through countless plots until we settled on one that had what we called a 'good vibe'. It was untamed, remote enough to feel like an escape and affordable enough to seem like a win.

In our excitement, we overlooked the three pillars of farming essentials: road access, water availability and electricity. The land itself was a wild, unruly sprawl of undergrowth—untouched, unstructured and just chaotic enough to convince us it had potential.

Unfortunately, enthusiasm doesn't run borewells, and good vibes don't make roads passable in the monsoon. The approach road was barely there, the soil was rebellious and the electricity connection turned into a several-month-long diplomatic exercise with the hamlet.

By the time we finally had water, a road of sorts and a single functioning switchboard, we had aged five years, emptied several savings accounts and learnt that rural infrastructure eats optimism for breakfast.

Tip:

Before you commit, check the basics. Access roads (or road-touch plots, as they are charmingly called), water sources and electricity availability are non-negotiable. Study the climate, rainfall patterns and proximity to towns for supplies. A plot with 'good vibes' is a lovely bonus, but it won't compensate for poor practicality.

2. Start with Small, Local Crops First

Our Experience:

In our rookie enthusiasm, we decided to aim high. Why settle for the ordinary when you could have fields of black rice swaying in the breeze, vegetables growing in neat rows like a Pinterest board and a mushroom operation that screamed sophistication? It was a bold plan—bold enough to raise the eyebrows of every villager within a ten-kilometre radius.

The black rice fared decently, but crops like bajra (pearl millet) taught us a humbling lesson about nature's sense of humour—what wasn't devoured by the birds seemed to vanish into thin air. As for the mushrooms, their brief reign was brought to an unceremonious end by an army of rogue mice who preferred their fungi al dente.

Tip:

When venturing into farming, start with simple, hardy crops that are already well-suited to your region's soil, climate and local conditions. Save your exotic crop dreams for small, experimental patches with lower stakes. Treat them as your side hustle while the mainstay crops keep your farming venture grounded (and productive).

3. Build Local Relationships

Our Experience:

When we first arrived in the village with our urban dreams of organic farming, we quickly realised that navigating rural life was like learning a new language—one where goodwill, patience and trust are the most valuable currency.

Enter key village leaders like the Police Patil and Sarpanch, who became our guides through the labyrinth of local bureaucracy and logistics. Their support helped us untangle everything from electricity permissions to land boundaries—things we naïvely thought could be sorted with a few emails and a can-do attitude.

Of course, none of this happened over formal meetings. Our most successful breakthroughs were often fuelled by strategically timed boxes of pedas and barfis. Call it 'mithai diplomacy'—a time-tested tradition of winning hearts (and support) one sweet at a time.

Tip:

In rural farming communities, no one cares about your spreadsheets. What matters is showing up, listening and remembering who likes their chai with extra sugar. A good conversation can do more than any plan on paper—and don't underestimate the power of a well-timed box of boondi ladoos. Generosity and respect will always open doors.

4. Show Up for the Community

Our Experience:

Farming, we discovered, isn't just about the land—it's about the people who live beside it. The hamlet watches: suspiciously, curiously and with the quiet caution of those who've seen city folk come and go. They want to know who you are, what you're up to and whether you'll stick around beyond your first harvest—or your first mishap.

In the early days, we were 'those city folk with the big ideas'. But we kept showing up—sometimes with seedlings, sometimes with sweets, occasionally with paracetamol and sachets of ORS during a heatwave. We chipped in supplies for the hamlet school, gave the kids notebooks and jackets when we could, and always stopped to chat when they called out, 'Madam! Madam!'

We began to see the quiet magic of simply showing up, sometimes for just five minutes, at village events. Jatras, school celebrations, Devi poojas, festivals. We often had no clue what was going on, but we stood there anyway, smiling, waving and clapping when everyone else did. Apparently, that counted.

Tip:

Show up—even if just for a token appearance. Celebrate with the community, not outside it. Offer help where you can, especially when no one is asking. You don't have to become a local overnight, but consistent small gestures—be it ORS packets, stationery for kids or showing your face at a festival—build the kind of goodwill no amount of money can buy. Farming might start with land, but it takes root in community.

5. Water and Power are Non-Negotiable

Our Experience:

Water and electricity are the lifeblood of any farm, but installing them felt like starring in our very own farming soap opera. Securing water began with the miracle of the coconut and ended in logistical chaos, while electricity brought its own drama—negotiations, delays and what we affectionately came to call the 'pole-tax' saga.

The process involved multiple visits, endless forms and more patience than we thought we possessed. Without either utility in place, our crop dreams remained just that—dreams.

Tip:

Sort out water and electricity before planting a single seed. For water, thoroughly test borewell sites and plan for alternative systems, such as rainwater harvesting. For electricity, confirm every detail with contractors, involve local leaders to smooth over concerns and budget for unexpected expenses. You'll need every drop of water and every volt of power to make things grow—starting with your patience.

6. The Bureaucracy Will Test You

Our Experience:

If farming is a test of your patience, then land registration is the advanced-level exam—complete with trick questions, disappearing paperwork and a chorus of touts and intermediaries. The registration office offered a masterclass in apathy and opportunism, made worse by the ever-present meddling of the Fiend. What got us through was the steady support of our unflappable local lawyer and the calm competence of our dynamic duo, M&S, who kept us sane when everything else conspired to do the opposite. Finally, clutching the 7/12 extract felt like lifting a hard-won trophy—proof that we'd survived the system and taken one real step closer to becoming farmers.

Tip:

Hire someone local who understands the intricacies of the system and has established relationships with the relevant individuals. Make a detailed checklist of permits and documents and stay organised. Bureaucracy may feel like a trial by fire, but treat it as part of your initiation into farming.

7. Infrastructure is a Lifeline

Our Experience:

When we first purchased our farmland, the thrill of sowing crops and nurturing the soil completely overshadowed the less glamorous need for infrastructure. We focused on planting and dreaming, leaving practical considerations like storage and protection for tools as distant afterthoughts.

Our access road, grandly named the 'Fiend Highway', soon betrayed us, turning into a muddy, treacherous mess every time the monsoons came. What started as a symbol of progress quickly became an obstacle course better suited to off-roading enthusiasts than farmers.

Meanwhile, left exposed to the elements, tools and machinery began a slow and steady descent into rusted oblivion. Tarps vanished. Power tools died. Fencing? Non-existent. Our romantic vision of farming was rapidly overtaken by the reality of watching hard work and investment washed away—sometimes literally.

Tip:

Plan for infrastructure early and allocate a generous budget. A good access road, secure storage, fencing and reliable irrigation systems are non-negotiable investments. Without them, even the best-laid farming plans can be flattened by the next rainstorm.

8. Hire Local, Manage Expectations

Our Experience:

Hiring locally was both a necessity and a steep learning curve. Our closest neighbour, the local politician, had brought in workers from Uttar Pradesh. The locals resented the outsiders, mutual mistrust festered and, if rumour is to be believed, the workers eventually ran away—possibly with the politician's tractor.

We took a different path. Enter Maruti—our farmhand, a paradox of charm, chaos and accidental brilliance. His productivity ran on what we came to call 'hamlet standard time'. Instructions were interpreted with ... personality. Urgency was a flexible concept. And yet, in the crucial moments, he showed up—sometimes with inventive solutions, sometimes with wide-eyed panic, but always with heart. Vandana, his quietly capable wife, soon became just as indispensable. Between them, they stitched together a support system we didn't even know we needed. When extra hands were required, Maruti would materialise with a small battalion—Vandana's extended family, cousins, neighbours and occasionally someone who might simply have been passing by but got roped in anyway. With time, they became the steady bridge between our city-bred efficiency and the rural rhythm we were slowly learning to respect.

Tip:

Hiring locals builds goodwill and stability—but set expectations early. Be specific, fair and patient. Build trust slowly, and understand that rural work rhythms are tied to weather, festivals and tradition—not your calendar.

9. Learn the Local Language

Our Experience:

Our Marathi was patchy at best when we bought the farm, and the minute a discussion wandered beyond greetings and gestures, we'd glance at Sunil for help. He became our unofficial interpreter long before he agreed to be our farmer-in-crime.

But Suzann and I persevered. We picked up words, stumbled through sentences and did our best to be understood. The effort was mostly appreciated—though it occasionally caused mass confusion. Like the time I cheerfully asked Vandana, 'Kay pernar?' thinking—incorrectly—that 'pernar' was Marathi for 'what will you wear?'. The correct word, as I later learnt, was 'ghalnar'. Unfortunately, 'pernar' sounded suspiciously close to 'peenar', which in Marathi means 'to drink'—as in (possibly) alcohol.

Vandana froze.

The entire field fell silent.

Then she blinked and said indignantly, 'Nothing at all,' which sent everyone into hysterics.

Sunil just rolled his eyes, the way only a husband who has survived years of my linguistic adventures can.

Over time, our Marathi has improved—painfully, incrementally and often unintentionally comically. But every now and then, I'll still mangle a verb, invent a new tense or confidently unleash a word that absolutely does not exist in the Marathi language. Those are the moments when Sunil simply exhales deeply, the picture of a man praying for strength.

Tip:

Learn the basics of the local language. It softens suspicion, builds rapport and prevents costly mistakes. You don't need fluency—just enough to be understood and to know when something's going awry.

10. Nature Writes Its Own Rules

Our Experience:

The monsoons turned our access road into a river. Wild boars ravaged our crops. Birds and pests seemed to have a sixth sense for ripeness. Every time we thought we had a handle on things, nature laughed.

Eventually, we stopped fighting and started adjusting. We learnt to observe, to adapt and to prepare—but never to assume.

Tip:

Farming requires flexibility, humility and a readiness to embrace surprises. Diversify your crops to reduce risks and spread out your chances of success. Accept that no amount of planning can override nature's unpredictability.

11. Double Your Budget (At Least)

Our Experience:

Nothing blows through a budget quite like a farm. Borewells, irrigation repairs, replanting after storms—even humble tool sheds found a way to morph into major expenses for us. Whatever number you had in mind? Add zeroes.

Tip:

Take whatever budget you've pencilled in for your farming dream—and double it. Then add a little extra for disappearing tarpaulins, sudden fence collapses and that one overpriced tool you're now convinced no farm can survive without—even if no one else knows what it actually does.

12. Celebrate Every Win

Our Experience:

Farming can be a relentless grind, but celebrating every success, no matter how small, kept our dream alive. From our first rice harvest to our triumph with the marinara sauce, these moments reminded us why we embarked on this crazy adventure.

Tip:

Celebrate every milestone, big or small. Farming is as much about the journey as the destination, and celebrating along the way keeps that journey meaningful and fulfilling.

13. Expect the Unexpected—Always

Our Experience:

Stray cattle, broken pumps, absent labourers, wild boars, unseasonal rain. Our to-do list never matched reality. Even rural festivals reshuffled our calendar. Plans dissolved. Machinery failed. And yet, somehow, we carried on.

Tip:

In farming, surprises are the rule, not the exception. Always assume things will take twice as long—and cost twice as much—as what you expect. Flexibility isn't just helpful; it's essential. If you're prepared for the chaos and embrace it as part of the experience, you'll save yourself a lot of stress. Farming isn't just about adapting to chaos—it's about finding joy in it.

14. Don't Farm for Profit Alone

Our Experience:

Yes, we expect this to be a viable business ... eventually. But it's far from easy. Equipment breaks. Crops fail. Prices fluctuate. Labour disappears. The profit margins are thin and the timelines are long.

And yet—there's joy in the process. A well-filled sack of rice, a compliment on our sauce, a crop that survives the season. These are the small, hard-won moments that keep us going.

Tip:

Of course any venture must make financial sense. But if you're farming solely for profit, prepare yourself for disappointment. The rewards are real—but they're slow, seasonal and often intangible. Do it with grit, with passion and with a willingness to grow something beyond numbers.

Epilogue: Lessons in Mud, Mithai and Madness

Sometimes, on a quiet evening, when the last of the sunlight glows over the hills and the smell of damp earth rises after a lazy drizzle, we find ourselves wondering how two city people ended up here—ankle-deep in mud, comparing compost ratios, arguing about drip-line fittings and learning lessons we never signed up for.

Nothing about the farm unfolded neatly. Nothing followed the rules in any handbook we'd read. It didn't care about our plans, our budgets or the tidy lists in our notebooks. And yet, somewhere between the chaos and the small victories, life here began stitching itself into ours in ways we hadn't expected.

What surprised us most wasn't the harvests or the storms or even the never-ending parade of animals determined to sabotage our best efforts—it was the people. The community that gathered around us, sometimes loudly, sometimes quietly, but always present.

And, for all its trials and unexpected lessons, the farm gave us something more, something we hadn't anticipated: community.

On evenings when we weren't contending with the elements or warding off pests, we'd drag out our plastic chairs beneath the mango trees and settle in. Grim Sanjay would appear with his permanently furrowed brow, Mahesh the entrepreneurial event-planner would launch into news from three villages away, and Maruti the Imp—always smiling, always apologising for something—would arrive with Vandana in tow, who would be peeling fruit with practised ease. Children from the hamlet darted around us, hands sticky from the lollipops we'd brought, their laughter rising and falling like a soundtrack the land had chosen for itself.

One evening, as we eased back into our seats, the air soft around us, I asked, almost casually, 'Do you really think the highway will be repaired by next December?'

Grim Sanjay scoffed. 'Sure. But which December?'

Maruti burst out laughing, while Vandana shook her head, peeling a mango and offering us slices.

The air smelled of ripe fruit, wet leaves and early nightfall—the kind of scent that makes you forget the city entirely.

We weren't rice magnates. We weren't model farmers. But under those trees, with turmeric dust still under my nails and the sound of children shrieking over a game I don't understand, I can't think of any other place I'd rather be.

It turned out that success wasn't measured in kilos of rice or the number of vegetables we salvaged, or even in how many times we failed and tried again. It lived in these small, unremarkable moments—the ease of shared laughter, the unspoken understanding with those who had lived on this land for far longer than we had, the feeling of being woven slowly into the rhythm of a place that didn't give itself easily.

Looking ahead, the farm remains—as always—unpredictable.

The weather will throw its tantrums.

The soil will test our patience.

The cows will almost certainly plot mischief.

We've stopped expecting it to get easier. We've learnt instead to meet each challenge as it comes, drawing from the land's quiet insistence to keep moving forward.

In the city, failure hides politely. On the farm, it is loud and immediate—announced through wilted leaves, chewed seedlings or in the unmistakable smugness of a bird who's eaten your best tomatoes. But it never lingers. The land doesn't allow it to. There is always another seed to plant, another season to prepare for, another chance to get it right—or at least less wrong.

And so we continue: a little wiser, a little more weather-beaten, a lot more entertained by the absurdity of it all.

The farm, with all its trials and triumphs, has rooted itself into our lives. It has tested us, changed us and taught us what resilience looks like when it's covered in mud. But more than anything, it has given us a place to belong—a place to grow, to stumble, to learn and to start again.

Seasons will keep shifting. The land will continue its endless cycle. And so will we.

Because no matter how unpredictable farming may be, one thing remains certain: there will always be another harvest, another lesson, and another reason to come back.

Acknowledgements

THEY SAY IT TAKES A VILLAGE, AND I'VE BEEN FORTUNATE to find mine in the most unexpected places.

This book would never have existed without Suzann, my farmer-in-crime, co-conspirator in chaos, and the one who casually said, 'Let's buy a farm,' and set this entire adventure in motion. Thank you for being the best possible partner on this wild, unpredictable ride. It's been quite something, and we're nowhere near done.

Sunil, my husband, my rock, and the eternally reluctant third wheel on our farm tricycle, thank you for your patience, humour and unwavering support. With you, I feel most like myself.

Kanan, my sister, my fiercest cheerleader and the first reader of every draft (including the ones that should never have seen daylight), thank you for always believing in me.

Dad, thank you for your unfiltered enthusiasm for all our farm misadventures and for braving those bone-rattling drives with a spirit that belies your age.

Maruti, Vandana, Sanjay and Mahesh, thank you for the toil, steadiness, resilience and problem-solving that held the farm, and us, together through every season. And the kids of the hamlet, your joy, curiosity and wide-open presence give the farm a heartbeat I carry with me.

To my girl squad—Priya, Archana and Maithili—gracias and hugs in equal measure.

Geeta Rao, you spotted a book quietly forming inside my scribbles long before I did.

Michelle, thank you for your steady encouragement, and for nudging me forward every time I stalled.

Lyndsay, thank you for accompanying Suzann on the farm hunt and helping identify the two plots at Mahagaon and Mahure.

Dinesh, thank you for the game-changing power tiller that ended our reliance on Vishwas and his bulls.

Thank you, Jayapriya at Jacaranda, for taking me on. And to Smita, my agent, thank you for championing the manuscript with such care.

To everyone at Westland, especially my commissioning editor, Aurodeep, thank you for the editorial rigour and for making this process far smoother than it had any right to be.

And to everyone who encouraged us, helped us, read my blogs, quietly rooted for this farm from near and far, and supported the work we do with the hamlet school and its children—thank you for being part of our village.